Guide

22

Così fan tutte

Mozart

Kiri te Kanawa as Fiordiligi in the 1981 production by John Copley at Covent Garden (photo: Clive Barda)

Preface

This series, published under the auspices of English National Opera and The Royal Opera, aims to prepare audiences to evaluate and enjoy opera performances. Each book contains the complete text, set out in the original language together with a current performing translation. The accompanying essays have been commissioned as general introductions to aspects of interest in each work. As many illustrations and musical examples as possible have been included because the sound and spectacle of opera are clearly central to any sympathetic appreciation of it. We hope that, as companions to the opera should be, they are well-informed, witty and attractive.

The Royal Opera is very grateful to The Baring Foundation for making possible the publication of this Guide to *Così fan tutte*.

Nicholas John
Series Editor

Così fan tutte

Wolfgang Amadeus Mozart

Opera Guide Series Editor: Nicholas John

Published in association with
English National Opera and The Royal Opera
and assisted by a generous donation
from The Baring Foundation

John Calder · London
Riverrun Press · New York

First published in Great Britain, 1983, by
John Calder (Publishers) Ltd,
18 Brewer Street,
London W1R 4AS

and

First published in the U.S.A., 1983, by
Riverrun Press Inc.,
175 Fifth Avenue,
New York, NY 10010

BRITISH LIBRARY CATALOGUING IN PUBLICATION DATA
Mozart, Wolfgang Amadeus
   Così fan tutte.—(Opera guide; 22)
   1. Mozart, Wolfgang Amadeus. Così fan tutte
   2. Operas—Librettos
   I. Title   II. Da Ponte, Lorenzo
   III. John, Nicholas   IV. Series
   782.1'092'4   ML410.M9

   ISBN 0-7145-3882-5

Library of Congress Catalogue Card Number 83-045247

John Calder (Publishers) Ltd., English National Opera and
The Royal Opera House, Covent Garden Ltd., receive
financial assistance from the Arts Council of Great Britain.
English National Opera also receives financial assistance from
the Greater London Council.

Typeset in Plantin by Margaret Spooner Typesetting, Dorchester, Dorset.

Printed and bound in Great Britain at The Camelot Press Ltd, Southampton

Contents

List of Illustrations

Mozart at the time of 'Così fan tutte'

Brian Trowell

Mozart conceived and composed *Così fan tutte* during the latter part of 1789. It was the last of his three Italian comedies to librettos by Lorenzo da Ponte and the last work that he wrote for the Emperor Joseph II's court opera company at the Burgtheater in Vienna; it was first performed there on January 26, 1790, on the eve of Mozart's thirty-fourth birthday. The opera enjoyed a moderate success and was soon performed in other South German and Austrian cities. From the first, however, it was regarded as a problematic work and was altered and adapted in various ways in order to soften, or at least make more plausible, the harsh lessons that were taught in da Ponte's 'School for Lovers'. Sir Thomas Beecham, in our own century, was the first to perform the piece 'straight', from a text faithful to Mozart's and da Ponte's intentions, and was vindicated by a remarkable series of performances in the early years of Glyndebourne which re-established *Così* in the general repertory. Although the opera has never lacked admirers and apologists, and has now been welcomed back into the Mozart canon, the thoughtful listener who is not dazzled by hero-worship cannot help feeling that certain problems remain. And when one is dealing with an artist of Mozart's stature, concerned with morality as well as feeling, a normally flawless stylist whose smiling charm conceals deep thought and human concern, one may be forgiven for presuming that unsolved problems in his art in some way reflect unsolved problems in his life. What are the problems in *Così fan tutte*?

Its subject-matter is very much in line with the themes of the earlier comedies, *The Marriage of Figaro* (1786) and *Don Giovanni* (Prague, 1787; Vienna, 1788), though *Così* does not present us with a picture of all classes of society, and the attack on aristocratic privilege is missing. Instead, the emphasis falls on innocence seduced and naiveté taught a lesson, on the contrast between the sentimental idealism of conventional young 'love' and the mysterious temptation and impersonal but compelling reality of desire. The education of the two pairs of lovers is conducted by an elderly cynic, with the help of a worldly maidservant. The strangeness and fascination of desire is symbolised by the *farouche* Albanian disguises that the two young men are made to adopt — at once ridiculous, curiously attractive and even, perhaps, threatening (Joseph II had only recently returned from a Balkan campaign against the Turks when he allegedly commissioned the opera). No doubt in order to distract attention from the central implausibility of these disguises, not to mention that of the lovers' final reconciliation, da Ponte served up the tale with a strong spice of pure farce — the maid disguising herself, even more ludicrously than the lovers, as an electro-magnetic doctor and as a tediously learned notary. In other places, such as Fiordiligi's 'simile aria' *Come scoglio* and the men's pretended suicide, da Ponte poked fun at the conventions, situations and sentiments of serious opera; and Mozart (much as he loved *opera seria*) was delighted to further his librettist's designs with clever musical parody — much of it, of course, lost on modern audiences.

As a result of all this, a dramatic idea that Sheridan would have treated as a serio-comic play, combining the stylised portrayal of manners and sentiment, emerges as an uneasy and unsettlingly mixed artistic experience, in which some of the truest and tenderest music that Mozart ever wrote co-exists with such dangerously empty pieces as the allegro of *Come scoglio*, with its tin trumpet and triplet scales rushing mechanically up and down, or the (for Mozart) merely *routinier* funny music of the Act One finale, so empty and meaningless when compared with the Act Two finale of *Figaro*.

It was not only deeply serious artists such as Beethoven and Wagner who were puzzled by this dubious artistic morality. Ordinary theatre folk were too. The string of adaptations, starting very soon after Mozart's death, tried to remove the more farcical elements in one way or another: by introducing two extra men as the Albanian tempters, or a manservant to dress up as the doctor and lawyer, for instance. The most extreme measure (short of Barbier and Carré fitting out the music with the plot of *Love's Labours Lost*) was to have Despina reveal Alfonso's plot to her mistresses early on, which removes the central and serious moral and leaves one with pure confectionery.

If *Così* is today an unquestioned success, it is perhaps because an affluent society has adopted a 'culinary' approach to opera not unlike that of the Viennese aristocracy whose tastes da Ponte well understood: opera has largely ceased to be a cultural growth-point, a forum where audiences welcome the artistic embodiment of contemporary issues and problems — however much this may enrage the avant-garde director. *Così* has become what it was not in Mozart's time, a remote costume-drama where *all* the characters wear fancy dress. We hero-worship Mozart and yield to the persuasions of his elegance; the supreme stylist has made us deaf to his occasional stylistic lapses. We have been very ready to follow the advocacy of E.J. Dent's famous book *Mozart's Operas*; but his elegant chapter on *Così* — significantly, the shortest in the book — simply does not discuss the problems inherent in the opera; and Dent had a notoriously low opinion of women.

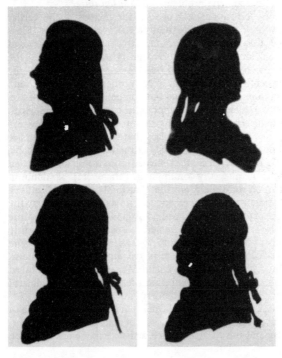

Silhouettes by Löschenkohl of the singers who created four of the principal roles in Vienna, 1790: Francesco Benucci (Guglielmo), Dorotea Bussani (Despina), Vincenzo Calvesi (Ferrando) and Francesco Bussani (Don Alfonso)

8

The celebrated 1944 Sadler's Wells production by Sacha Montov, designed by Kenneth Green. Left to right: John Hargreaves (Guglielmo), Joan Cross (Fiordiligi), Rose Hill (Despina), Owen Brannigan (Don Alfonso), Margaret Ritchie (Dorabella) and Peter Pears (Ferrando). (photo: Alexander Bender)

Why should Mozart have produced such an equivocal opera in 1789? The period after *Don Giovanni* was a time of increasing difficulty in his life. He held a court appointment, but his imperial master asked him to compose nothing but ballroom dances, and was paying him little. He was not in the best of health, and his wife fell so ill that she had to go to Baden for an expensive water-cure. He had few pupils to teach. The concerts for which he composed the last three symphonies had to be abandoned for lack of subscribers, so that he probably never heard what he must have known were his greatest essays in the form.

In an attempt to earn some extra money he undertook a northern tour in April, May and June of 1789, going via Prague, Dresden and Leipzig to Berlin, where he greatly impressed the music-loving Frederick William II (who had succeeded his famous uncle Frederick the Great in 1786). But although the King commissioned a set of string quartets for himself (as an able cellist) and some easy piano sonatas for his daughter, there is no evidence that he offered Mozart permanent employment, and Mozart was slow to fulfil his commissions. Admired and fêted, he must have been reminded of his brilliant childhood tours as an infant prodigy; but this time there were only small rewards. He wrote to his wife that she would have to welcome him back for himself alone, not because he brought any money with him.

His main profit was to increase his knowledge of the music of J.S. Bach at St Thomas's in Leipzig, to renew old acquaintanceships — accompanying his friend the soprano Josepha Duschek in arias from *Figaro*, for example — and to hear his *Die Entführung aus dem Serail (The Seraglio)* in Berlin. The part of Blonde was taken by the beautiful and gifted Henriette Baranius, who asked Mozart to coach her privately; Rochlitz tells us that the susceptible composer fell completely under her spell, and that his friends had the greatest difficulty in prising him loose from her clutches.

Mozart, it seems, well understood the call of desire that led Dorabella and Fiordiligi to fall (the first easily, the second only after grief and heartbreak). Did his wife Konstanze get to hear of it? She fell ill immediately after Mozart's return to Vienna, and the cost of her medical treatment and stay in Baden plunged Mozart into terrible financial difficulties, as his despairing, dunning letters to the merchant and fellow-Mason Puchberg reveal. No sooner had Konstanze started to recover, though, than she began to flirt and behave, apparently, with considerable immodesty with a man who was kind enough to let Mozart know about it (but she later scored his name out of the letter of anguished reproach that Mozart wrote to her). The affair may or may not have been serious, but it was precisely this reputation for giddy behaviour that had led Mozart's father and sister to oppose Mozart's marriage in the first place. Mozart may have lapsed from fidelity himself, but his letter to Konstanze of early August 1789 shows a man extremely jealous as well as apprehensive for his wife's honour: 'I'd wish, sometimes, that you didn't make yourself so common ... Remember the promises that you made me, Oh God! ... Don't torment yourself and me with unnecessary jealousy ... Only the wise behaviour of a wife can lay chains on a husband ... Don't ever go alone [to the baths] — I am terrified at the thought.' The letter elsewhere suggests that Mozart was having to prove his own good faith: 'have confidence in my love, you already have proofs of it — and you will see how contented we shall be.' Just as Mozart was about to begin work on *Così fan tutte*, then, we find him up to the neck in a marital crisis. The cynical Don Alfonso would have noted that the pair had been married for just seven years: time for the proverbial itch to make itself felt. I suspect that this situation, which was not of the kind to resolve itself quickly, threw Mozart off balance just at the time when he would have been discussing the idea of *Così* with da Ponte. The result was a work in which moments of unsurpassed tenderness or anguish (the farewells and *Terzettino* of Act One, Fiordiligi's *'Per pietà'* and her moment of yielding in Act Two) sit very uneasily alongside the elements of farce and the glossed-over final reconciliation.

We know very little about the commissioning and first ideas for *Così*. Da Ponte hardly mentions the opera in his memoirs. *Figaro* was revived at the court opera in August 1789, and in July Mozart was writing two substitute arias for the new Susanna to sing. Doubtless the successful revival led to the commission, which, Niemetschek implies, came from the Emperor himself. Heinse, a less authoritative source, tells us that Joseph also suggested the story, which had its origin in an actual escapade of the time. The basic situation, and of course many of the elements of farce and parody, can be paralleled in a number of earlier operas and plays, but it would seem that da Ponte, that superb arranger and adapter, was here responsible for the whole conduct of the plot. Mozart must have asked for a great many ensembles, for there are more in *Così* even than in *Figaro*; the permutations and combinations of the pairs of lovers and the two masters-of-ceremonies, Alfonso and Despina, allow of a remarkable variety.

We can be sure that both Mozart and da Ponte took fully into account the capabilities of their singers and also, as I shall suggest, their weaknesses too. The Fiordiligi, Adriana Ferrarese del Bene, was at the time da Ponte's mistress. Mozart did not much admire her when he first heard her in Dresden in April 1789: 'Madame Allegranti is far better than Madame Ferrarese, which I admit is not saying much'. She was, as her name declares, born in Ferrara (as were the sisters in *Così*, an in-joke by da Ponte) in about 1755. She was therefore thirty-five in 1790. At fifteen, as a talented pupil of Sacchini in the Ospedaletto in Venice, she had been heard with some admiration by Dr Burney. He noted that she 'had a very extraordinary compass of voice, as she was able to reach the highest E of our harpsichords [a semitone beneath the

Viorica Ursuleac as Fiordiligi (Royal Opera House Archives)

Queen of Night's top F], upon which she could dwell a considerable time, in a fair, natural voice'. Burney confuses Adriana, whose surname was Gabrieli, with Francesca Gabrielli, sister of the famous soprano Caterina Gabrielli; Francesca, who must have been born in Rome, like her sister an illegitimate daughter of Prince Gabrielli, would have been about thirty-five in 1770, and cannot possibly, as Scholes points out, have been the 'orphan girl' that Burney heard. The question of Adriana's sister comes up again in the history of *Così*, for Haydn's biographer, Pohl, in an account of the Italian opera company in Vienna that is quite peripheral to his main story, states that Louise (Luisa, Aloisia) Villeneuve, who sang Dorabella, was Adriana's sister. He gives no evidence, and is possibly relying on some confused memory of Burney's mistake.

Adriana was no great beauty, and at the time of *Così* no youngster either, but da Ponte tells us that she had fine eyes and a beautiful mouth. She was apparently not a good actress. Parke, who heard her in 1785 in London, said that she had 'a sweet voice and sang with taste' [i.e. she was a mistress of the ornamental, florid style], but 'was not calculated to shine as a *prima donna*'; even so, she was 'much applauded'. Her abilities in the high style, when she came to sing Susanna in the revival of *Figaro*, led Mozart to revive an old idea, originally abandoned, to give Susanna a noble, *opera seria* aria to sing in the garden in her disguise as the Countess. In 1789 this replaced *Deh vieni*. If Adriana were not a dextrous actress, she would have found the 'dressing-up' aria in Act Two of *Figaro* a problem also: this appears to have been replaced with the charming but dramatically neutral arietta *Un moto di gioia*. Mozart said of the latter that he thought it would please the audience (as it had pleased her), 'always providing that she is capable of singing it naively': *naiv* may have meant 'unornamented', but if he only meant 'simply' or 'artlessly', that may have been a further reason for his excising *Deh vieni*, which does not require the kind of showmanship that la Ferrarese excelled in.

In *Così*, her freakishly wide compass and capacity for mannered singing are exploited to the full: parodistically in *Come scoglio*, sincerely in *Per pietà*. Her part is not a comic one, save by the irony of the situation, and evidently should not be guyed. According to da Ponte (whatever Parke may have said), she had all the off-stage qualities of the legendary *prima donna*, 'a somewhat impetuous nature, calculated to provoke the malevolent rather than to attract friends'. It was her factiousness and love of teasing her rivals that led to her dismissal from the company shortly after *Così*, and consequently to da Ponte's too, for he rashly tried to protect her. Would we have had a further Mozart/da Ponte collaboration if she and her lover had been wiser?

About Louise Villeneuve we know very little. If she were indeed Adriana's sister, there would have been more point to da Ponte's joke about the 'dame ferraresi' ('ladies from Ferrara'). Pohl says that she was one of the greatest beauties of her time, again without stating his evidence. Mozart, perhaps wishing to test what she could do, composed three fine arias for her to insert into other men's operas during August and October 1789. She had sung in Vienna since 1788, singing Amor to Adriana's Diana in da Ponte's *Arbore di Diana*. The *Wiener Zeitung* said that she 'was justly applauded for her charming appearance, her subtle, expressive acting and her artistically beautiful singing'. Certainly Dorabella has a more varied part in *Così* than Fiordiligi. Though the vocal athletics are less demanding, she has to command a greater variety of styles of singing, and as an actress to make credible the change from angry protestation to flighty enjoyment of her new admirer. Louise vanishes from history even before Adriana, whom we last meet in a sad,

Blanche Thebom as Dorabella (Royal Opera House Archives)

sour interview in da Ponte's pages in 1799.

As in the case of *Don Giovanni*, Mozart could call on the services of a leading Italian tenor for *Così*: Vincenzo Calvesi, who had arrived in Vienna in April 1785 after recent successes in Parma and Venice. Mozart had heard him, no doubt, in his friend Stephen Storace's two operas (one with a da Ponte libretto), and had written ensembles for Bianchi's *La villanella rapita*, in which Calvesi sang in November 1785. He continued as a leading lyric tenor in Vienna, with some absences, until 1794. A review of 1790 describes him as 'one of the best tenors from Italy, who combines a voice naturally sweet, pleasant and sonorous with a technique which, without being mannered or over-cultivated, never fails to please our public' (trans. Christopher Raeburn). As Ferrando, he paired well with the serious Fiordiligi: his main experience lay in the 'serious' parts for star-crossed lovers that were normal in comic opera. He was the highest tenor that Mozart ever composed for (the parts that Storace wrote for him also require an unusual upper register): though Ferrando needs a round, firm bottom D in *Un' aura amorosa* (a parody which Mozart, thank heaven, set seriously), he has to negotiate no less than thirteen high B-flats in *Ah, lo veggio*, which is therefore frequently omitted.

Stronger acting was required of Mozart's Guglielmo, Francesco Benucci (*c*1745-1824), one of the very finest bass-baritones of his age and very well known to Mozart as his first Figaro and Leporello. He was as good an actor as he was a singer. He made his debut in Pistoia, apparently, in 1769, was the leading *buffo* in Venice in 1778-9, and enjoyed a huge success in Milan between 1779 and 1782. He came to Vienna briefly in 1783, when Mozart heard him: 'The *buffo* is particularly good — his name is Benucci', he wrote, and planned a part for him in his abortive *Lo sposo deluso* (in which Francesco Bussani, Mozart's Don Alfonso, was also to have figured). Benucci performed all over Europe, and seems to have sung, with Nancy Storace (reputedly his mistress for a time), the first Mozart ever heard on the London stage: the duet *Là ci darem la mano*, from *Don Giovanni*. He is by far the best-known of Mozart's singers, and I need not repeat here in full the often-quoted account, from Michael Kelly's reminiscences, of Mozart saying 'Bravo, bravo Benucci!' as the singer electrified the cast and orchestra at a rehearsal of *Figaro* with his singing of 'Cherubino alla vittoria!' in *Non più andrai*. He possessed 'a very round, beautiful, full bass voice', and was noted for his subtle underplaying of *buffo* roles. Choron thought him the ideal of what a singer should be. Unlike most *buffo* singers, he was equally good in serious roles. Mozart seems to have valued his heroic potentialities highly, and wrote an aria for him as Guglielmo, *Rivolgete a lui lo sguardo*, which was too big for its context, so that he replaced it with the present *Non siate ritrosi*. The climax of the rejected aria recalls Count Almaviva rather than Figaro, but the driving misogyny of *Aprite up po' quegl' occhi* surfaces again in Guglielmo's insistent *'ma, quel farlo a tanti e tanti'*, which is anything but a joke.

The remaining two singers in *Così* were man and wife, and it is interesting that Mozart and da Ponte had every reason to dislike them. Don Alfonso, the ageing cynic, was taken by Francesco Bussani, who curiously enough had been cast as an elderly 'sprezzator di donne' in *Lo sposo deluso*. Born in Rome in 1743, he had settled in Vienna not only as a singer, but also as a stage-manager. Da Ponte tells us that he was 'master of every trade save that of an honest man', and that it was Bussani who tried to ruin *Figaro* by getting the authorities to refuse to allow dancers to be used for the Fandango scene. Mozart never wrote an aria for him outside the parts of Bartolo/Antonio and the Commendatore/Masetto (in each case he doubled roles). He had a

Christa Ludwig (Dorabella) and Pilar Lorengar (Fiordiligi) at the Deutsche Oper, Berlin

generous ('ausgebend') bass voice, but it was evidently weak in the lower register, since Mozart does not normally put him on the bass-line in ensembles. His officious, gobbling turkey-cock manner is probably parodied in Bartolo's *La vendetta*. By the time of *Così* he may have been losing his powers of sustaining a line (he was 47), since Mozart gives Don Alfonso no proper aria.

Bussani's wife, Dorotea, though her maiden name was Sardi, was in fact Austrian. She had sung Cherubino, but never another note by Mozart except the role of Despina. Da Ponte disliked her intensely, saying that she won her following by grimaces and clown's tricks, and suggesting too that her infidelities gave her husband, who was twenty years older, a dog's life. Some accounts suggest that she was more actress than singer, with a very attractive physique, but there were those who admired her voice: a witness in 1790 thought he had never heard 'such beautiful and charming chest voice, nor one used with such good humour and so mischievously' (as Fidalma in Cimarosa's *The Secret Marriage*). This tallies well with Despina's arias, where Mozart's musical charms beautify rather worldly sentiments. One wonders whether the personalities of this pair, and their love of intrigue, had anything to do with the way da Ponte and Mozart conceived their functions in *Così*. . .

Florence Easton as Fiordiligi. This English soprano sang regularly at the Met. from 1917 to 1929 (photo: Mishkin, N.Y.)

A Commentary on the Score

H.C. Robbins Landon

Like all Mozart's mature operas, *Così* also begins and ends in the principal key — in this case, C major. In the eighteenth century, composers usually wrote the Overture (*sinfonia* in Italian) after the opera proper had been completed; and that was apparently the procedure here, so that Mozart could, in the *Andante* introduction prepare us for the 'motto' theme of the work:

(Andante)

Co – sì   fan   tut – te

And where do the words come from? An unimpeachable source, to wit, *The Marriage of Figaro*, Act One, the terzetto between Susanna, Don Basilio and the Count, in which Cherubino has overheard the Count making love to Susanna, and the Count takes Cherubino to task for trying to seduce the peasant-girl Barbarina. Don Basilio, the sophisticated cynic, sings *'Così fan tutte le belle, non c'è alcuna novità'* ('That's what they all do, the ladies, there's nothing new in that').

(Allegro assai)
BASILIO

Co-sì   fan tut-te   le   bel-le; non c'è al-cu —na   no – vi – tà

Ryland Davies (Ferrando), Paolo Montarsolo (Don Alfonso) and Knut Scram (Guglielmo) in the 1969 Glyndebourne production by Franco Enriquez, designed by Luzzati (photo: Guy Gravett)

Dorabella (Della Jones) bids farewell to Ferrando (Anthony Rolfe-Johnson) at ENO, 1981 (photo: Donald Southern)

Not only do the words form the title of the new opera, *Così fan tutte*, but when Basilio repeats the words

that undulating phrase in quavers will become part of *Così fan tutte*'s Overture:

This quotation forms part of the *Presto* (main) section of the Overture; but before we arrive at that point, the '*Così fan tutte*' motto is answered (as it will be when it reappears vocally in No. 30 just before the work's final *dénouement*) by the full orchestra. Then suddenly we are in the *Presto*, the music chattering away like an Italian *sinfonia* by Giovanni Paisiello or Domenico Cimarosa (but with Mozart's grander orchestration, the horns cleverly pitched in G* so that they are immediately ready to plunge into No. 1, which is in G, without

---

* Until Beethoven's death, horns were without valves and thus able to play only a limited number of notes on the harmonic scale. Horns in G were able to play triads in G and the diatonic scale upwards from g' to (about) g''; horns in C *basso*, which Mozart mostly used (as opposed to C *alto*, an octave higher), began their diatonic scale at c'. Changing the crooks in order to move to a different pitch took a certain amount of time, and by pitching the horns in G in a piece in C, Mozart could use them fully in the dominant (G) and plunge without stopping into the next piece of music, in the key of G.

Janet Baker as Dorabella ('Smanie implacabili') in the Scottish Opera production

having to change crooks and thus hold up matters on the stage). The alternating woodwind figures, which as we have seen come from *Figaro*, slyly suggest the intrigue to come, sliding from key to key and sounding slightly brittle and uncompromising. This Overture has always been a popular concert piece.

Act One

Così breaks sharply with the Italian tradition (as did *Figaro* four years before) in starting with not one but four ensembles — three trios and a duet. The usual pattern of an Italian composer would have been an aria followed by other arias and secco recitatives. *Così* does not have a proper aria (for No. 5 is so rapid as to be over almost before we know it) until No. 11 (Dorabella's aria *'Smanie implacabili'* 'Cease not, remorseless love' [5]), and a fast pace is ensured by three *allegro* ensembles one after another. The tonal scheme that Mozart employs for this series of numbers is unusual in that we veer sharply away from the home key but then return to it *and* a surprisingly full orchestration with trumpets and kettledrums in No. 3:

FERRANDO/*No. 3 Terzetto*

Lois McDonall (Fiordiligi) and Alan Opie (Guglielmo) in the 1978 revival at ENO (photo: Mike Humphrey)

In all this, the music is celebrating the lovers' certainty of their fiancées and Don Alfonso's cynical disbelief in their constancy. Their enclosed world is thus also projected tonally: the music has progressed in a third-related fashion, from G to E to C, and the process is now continued when, for the first time, the ladies appear on the scene.

Mozart's favourite orchestration of clarinets, horns and bassoons brings us to A major, a third below C. The new tonal scheme is:

Thus, rounder orchestration and flat (i.e. softer) keys represent the ladies, and the score, without oboes, trumpets or timpani, underlines the feminine domination of events on the stage. The two ladies, secure in their love for their respective gentlemen, are disturbed by Don Alfonso's news of their fiancés' immediate departure; and Mozart illustrates this musically by confronting A major with F minor. Ferrando and Guglielmo must leave for the wars — the first deception — and in No. 8 the full orchestra and a switch to the brilliant and martial key of D major [4] announce their imminent removal from civilian life.

With No. 9, the Quintet *'Di scrivermi ogni giorno'* ('You'll write long letters often'), we have a poignant farewell scene between the lovers, with Alfonso making fun of them to the audience (*'io crepo se non rido'* lit. I'll burst if I don't laugh), broken off by the second martial announcement (in D), summoning the officers to their ships. In the music up to now we have witnessed a gradual shifting of the tonal centre from the masculine world of the opening numbers, through the purely feminine world of No. 4 and a series of mixed ensembles, to the departure of the officers. At this point, da Ponte and Mozart introduce a definite cæsura and cause Fiordiligi, Dorabella and Don Alfonso to sing the hauntingly beautiful terzettino, *'Soave sia il vento'* ('O wind gently blowing')

The first deception is now completed and, as if to underline the betrayal of the two girls, Mozart writes music of peculiarly searching depth. The grand lie is celebrated by the most truthful music of which Mozart is capable: thus he is openly on the side of the angels (that is, the ladies), not (as would more cynical Italian composers) the deceivers.

In the second part of this new situation, Despina enters the scene: as an accomplice of Don Alfonso she too seeks to undermine the girls' steadfastness. In No. 11 [5], Dorabella has an agitated aria bemoaning her fate, but the gentle key of E flat and the 'soft' instrumentation (woodwind without oboes) begin to

'Soave sia il vento': Richard Van Allan with Kiri te Kanawa (Fiordiligi) and Agnes Baltsa (Dorabella) at Covent Garden in 1981 (photo: Clive Barda)

Denis Dowling (Don Alfonso) and Sheila Armstrong (Despina) in the 1965 Sadler's Wells production by Glen Byam Shaw (photo: Reg Wilson)

tell us that she is the weaker and more compliant of the two heroines. Mozart has begun to flesh out the sharply different character of his two leading ladies. Despina's aria (No. 12) [6] paints her as a cynical judge of the world in general and men in particular. As the plot thickens, there is gradually something slightly more than cynical about the purpose of Don Alfonso and his accomplice. They seem determined to destroy the lovers' idealism, indeed to reduce love to flirtation. They are almost serpents in the garden of Eden, deliberately destroying the innocence of the two couples. The innately sinister and evil aspect of this purpose lurks behind the particularly radiant music in which all this deception is couched.

The second deception is the arrival of the two lovers disguised as Turks, and the grand Sextet (No. 13), in which this is portrayed, musically unites all six protagonists for the first time together; as if to underline the musical importance of the gesture, we return to the original key of C major and to most of the original orchestration of the Overture (with its clarinets, trumpets and kettledrums). Characteristically Dorabella is the first to find the appearance of the 'Turks' intriguing *'che sembianze! che vestiti! che figure! che mustacchi!'*

(lit. What appearances! What clothes! What faces! What moustaches!). But the members of the mischievous quartet (Don Alfonso, Despina and the two 'Turks') have not yet succeeded in undermining the ladies — and indeed Ferrando and Guglielmo hope that the ruse will fail.

Mozart has organised the opera up to now with its tonal base in C major, ending with the Sextet (No. 13):

Overture —————————⟶ No. 3 Terzetto —————————⟶ No. 13 Sextet. From now on, innocence will begin to waver and C major totally disappears until the crucial duet in Act Two (No. 29, basic key: A major), in the middle of which the steadfast Fiordiligi admits having 'fallen' completely: *'Taci, ahime, son abbastanza tormentata, ed infelice'* (lit. Silence, alas, I am tormented and unhappy enough), when Ferrando threatens to take his life with a dagger:

FIORDILIGI

Ta - ci.., ahi - me, son ab-ba-stan-za tor - men-ta-ta,ed in - fe - li - ce!

That the central key of C is thus briefly touched upon (for we soon proceed back to A major) stresses the fact that we are gradually making our way back to the beginning: in No. 30 in C the cynical motto of the opera is proclaimed.

But innocence, in Fiordiligi's celebrated B flat aria (No. 14, *'Come scoglio'* i.e. rock-like), is not only defended but affirmed, to which end we have firm dotted figures but also

Andante maestoso

FIORDILIGI

(*f*)

Co — me scoglio

trumpets — one of their rare uses in that key in Mozart: others will occur, characteristically, when the men pretend, in the first Finale (No. 18) to take

Daniela Mazzucato (Despina) and Donald Gramm (Don Alfonso) at Covent Garden in 1978 (photo: Christina Burton)

Lois McDonall (Fiordiligi), Cynthia Buchan (Dorabella), Alan Opie (Guglielmo) and John Winfield (Ferrando) (photo: Mike Humphrey)

poison, and later when they awake after having been given the 'antidote'. The ladies cannot resist, and not only the trumpets mock their original metaphoric purpose, the strings *reverse* the dotted rhythm of *'Come scoglio'* and now play in 'Lombard' patterns (as they are termed):

coming *down* the scale ('fallen virtue') instead of going up, as previously, when her determination was 'rock-like'. In Ferrando's aria No. 24 (*'Ah lo veggio: quell'anima bella'* 'Well I know that a spirit of beauty'), when he acknowledges defeat (or, in Don Alfonso's terms, victory) — *'Ah, cessate, speranze fallici'* (lit. Ah, cease false hopes) — we again have B flat trumpets, previously 'rocks' of sturdy instrumentation, again utterly repudiating their original metaphoric purpose.

When Ferrando and Guglielmo were called off to the wars, their departure (i.e. transformation into 'Turks') was in D, so that when the 'Turks' are in the full swing of their amatory attempts, in the Finale of Act One (No. 18), to seduce their ladies in false partnership, Mozart swings round to D, in which key the Act concludes. But when the lovers went off to war their ladies were still steadfast, and even now, their fall is only suggested, for they are still resisting.

24

Anthony Rolfe-Johnson (Ferrando) and Alan Opie (Guglielmo) in the 1981 ENO production (photo: Donald Southern)

Hermann Prey (Guglielmo) and Rudiger Wohlers (Ferrando) at Covent Garden in 1979 (photo: Christina Burton)

Della Jones (Dorabella), Marilyn Hill Smith (Despina) and Felicity Lott (Fiordligi) at ENO (photo: Donald Southern)

Act Two

By the beginning of Act Two, however, the ladies are ripe for the fall, and for this love music Mozart returns to flat keys. The great wind band serenade in No. 21 (Duet with Chorus) is organized after the D major conclusion of Act One, as follows:

No. 19 Aria (Despina) in G, Despina's worldly wisdom;

No. 20 Duet (Fiordiligi, Dorabella) in B flat, wherein the ladies decide to take new lovers;

No. 21 Duet (Ferrando, Guglielmo) and Chorus, E flat.

Thus this grand seduction scene is prepared by the third-related keys G to B flat (the natural 'leading' dominant of E flat). In order to make all this credible, Mozart must write music of profound eroticism and passion, and to do so he chooses the wind band serenade (flutes, clarinets, bassoons, horns) in which he had already created a peculiarly personal and highly original series of works after arriving in Vienna (1781): not only are the Serenades in C minor (K. 388) and E flat (K. 375) a previous part of this great legacy but, more immediately, the most far-reaching, that for thirteen wind instruments (K. 361), now considered to date from c. 1784. Mozart had also previously introduced such serenade effects into his piano concertos (for instance in the slow movement of K. 482) where the piano is actually completely silent. Now, *mutatis mutandis*, the voices are silent as the lovers prepare cruelly to seduce the 'wrong' girls:

In the following quartet No. 22, Mozart further increases our (and the girls') gullibility by writing enchanting D major music punctuated by soft trumpets, as Don Alfonso unites the false lovers and then, in a tiny conclusion of whispering intrigue, he and Despina sneak away, leaving the lovers in their amorous deception. Dorabella and Guglielmo sing a rapturous duet (No. 23) [11] in which Guglielmo gently removes the miniature of Ferrando from her bosom and substitutes his own miniature talisman (a heart) instead.

Fiordiligi's turn comes in her famous Rondò (No. 25), with its virtuoso horn parts — of course horns, symbol of sexual betrayal and known to all Mozart lovers from Act Four of *Figaro*:

già o-gnu-no lo sa.

Here in *Così* the horns are often very exposed and treacherously difficult, as exposed as the treachery to which Fiordiligi has been brought: as she sings of her (new) faithful love, *'A chi mai mancò di fede . . .'* (lit. To whom I will never lack faith) the horns tell us that all is a farce:

(can-)dor, ca – ro   be – – – – ne al
(tuo candor.)

This was a bravura aria for Adriana del Bene, who was by this time da Ponte's mistress . . .

Anna Pollak (Dorabella) and Frederick Sharp (Guglielmo) in the 1944 Sadler's Wells production (photo: Angus McBean)

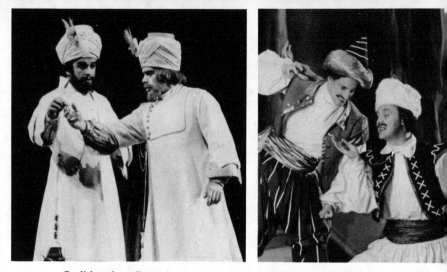

Guglielmo shows Ferrando what he has been given: (left) Alan Opie and Anthony Rolfe-Johnson (1981) (photo: Catherine Ashmore); (right) Peter Pears and John Hargreaves (1944) (photo: Alexander Bender)

The rage of the men knows no bounds: Ferrando fumes in an accompanied recitative when Guglielmo, maliciously, tells how he plucked Ferrando, as it were, from Dorabella's fair bosom; in No. 26, Guglielmo can afford to sing an aria, *'Donne mie, le fatte a tante'* ('Ladies have such variations'). Mozart reveals a moment of truth when, to the words *'m'avvilisce in verità'* (lit. it disheartens me in truth), we suddenly swerve into the key of C, not heard since No. 13 — which when it finally returns will be the key (i.e. moment) of truth. Ferrando then has a mournful accompanied recitative and Cavatina in C minor (the other side of truth i.e. C major) [14], *'Tradito, schernito dal perfido cor'* (lit. Betrayed, marked by the treacherous heart). The heart traduced poignantly introduces itself with a hint of the wind band serenade in E flat:

Everything has gone wrong (or, for Don Alfonso and Despina, right). The mocking wind band serenade is also prominent in Dorabella's 'love' aria No. 28 [15], where the beginning is like a blurred mirror of the seduction scene. We are still in flat keys, the magic circle of love.

Fiordiligi who resisted harder has consequently fallen harder: in her duet (No. 29) with Ferrando, of which we have spoken above, she cannot withstand the erotic music which Ferrando now directs towards her.

28

It is almost a paraphrase of the seduction scenes in *Don Giovanni*: for example, the celebrated Terzetto No. 15, which is also in A major, Leporello, disguised as Don Giovanni, woos Elvira while Don Giovanni laughs at the cruel deception. And Fiordiligi falls; Don Alfonso has won, and he celebrates his total victory over the chagrined losers of the bet in No. 30, when we return to C major and the brilliant Finale.

The key structure of this concluding set piece closely follows the action on the stage. The lavish wedding feast and its preparations plunge us into festive C major with the full orchestra including clarinets, trumpets and kettledrums. When the infatuated ladies appear, everything switches to *Andante* in E flat (also full orchestra), which in turn brings us to A flat and the fervent declaration of love between the (reversed) pairs. In a breathtaking enharmonic modulation we suddenly find ourselves in E major as Don Alfonso enters to tell the infatuated couples that the notary is about to arrive (the notary being, of course, the disguised Despina). (In a brilliantly satirical section, Mozart creates a huge dissonance in the wind parts which resolve themselves in an antiquated manner, to accompany the words *'colle regole ordinarie'* (lit. according to the prescribed rules).

Sadler's Wells, 1963: Donald McIntyre (Guglielmo), Catherine Wilson (Dorabella), Thomas Hemsley (Don Alfonso), Iris Kells (Despina), Heather MacMillan (Fiordiligi) and John Wakefield (Ferrando) (photo: Donald Southern)

All is ready for the double marriage when the music stops for an instant, before plunging into the D major march which sent the original officers off to the Turkish wars.*

Back to an agitated E flat, the 'Turks' disappear, to be replaced, to the consternation of the ladies, by the real Ferrando and Guglielmo. The dénouement takes place in a change from E flat to B flat as Despina reveals herself as the false notary and the betrayed ladies are displayed as betrayers. A return to E flat accompanies the mens' rage; they return, half in their Turkish disguises, to tease in sadistic fashion the ladies they have so successfully betrayed. The plot is revealed, the ladies taken back to their original lovers and the music, underlining the return to the beginning, itself returns to the principal key of C. But all is, of course, not well, as the music (and words) tell us, as Mozart quietly and ominously moves into F minor, *'Quel che suole altrui far piangere fia per lui cagion di riso'* (lit. What makes another weep is, for him, an occasion for laughter). In a last brilliant section, *Così* closes in all the glory of Mozart's C major symphonic style, reminiscent of the great 'Jupiter' Symphony composed two years before (K. 551).

Thus, in this extraordinary tour-de-force, we have looked backwards and forwards to the work's central key, while encompassing E flat (key of love), E major (key of the trio No. 2 in Act One when the betrayal is launched — hence the key of the notary in Act Two when the betrayal should be consummated) and of course D major (the march to the wars in Act One). It is a perfect and cruel symmetry.

Da Ponte was a great cynic, as his *Memoirs* show, and no doubt he intended *Così fan tutte* to be a momumentally cynical opera, as even the subtitle must indicate, *'Thus do all women or The School for Lovers'*. Only that Mozart,

---

* Mozart seems to have assumed that *Così fan tutte* took place in 1789 and therefore the war that Austria was waging was actually against Turkey.

at least in many critics' opinion, has removed a great deal of the cynicism. In the previous operas on which da Ponte and Mozart collaborated, *The Marriage of Figaro* and *Don Giovanni*, two of the pillars were love and forgiveness, the deepest love and the deepest forgiveness of which human beings are capable. Now in *Così fan tutte*, when the lovers return and unmask themselves, we are confronted with Mozart's (and da Ponte's) greatest act of forgiveness. Perhaps the whole perfidy can never be forgiven, for all four — or rather all six, including Despina and Don Alfonso — are equally guilty of a gross act of deception, but more — of traducing love. Can that ever be forgiven?

Recently* Bernard Levin has broadcast some perceptive remarks on *Figaro*. He has equally perceptive things to say about *Don Giovanni, The Magic Flute* and *Così*. He says, 'somehow it seems that most Mozart lovers do have a particular preference among the four.'

And since each of the four operas has its own quality, which is clearly differentiated from the qualities of the other three, I do not think it is too odd a fancy to suppose that each of the four is loved best by people who respond to its particular quality ... [As for *Don Giovanni*] it is the romantics among us, and also, even more I think, those who secretly yearn to be among that bright, brave band but dare not, who respond most readily to the operatic Don Giovanni, a man who, even while giving orders for a party, is thinking of the women he will conquer at it ...; [while as for *The Magic Flute*] it breathes wisdom, peace and a grave certainty, and those whose hopes of heaven are sure, will be carried along in ecstasy on its broad river to the apotheosis of its ending. But amid the nobility and profundity of *The Magic Flute* something is crowded out: it is the fully human response to the fully human situation ... [Concerning *Figaro*, we read that] it seems to me to constitute the pinnacle of Mozart's achievement, precisely because it is the most personal and intimate of these four masterpieces .... It speaks of love ... in phrases of melting beauty, of purity and innocence, of unselfishness and rapture, of — above all — humanity, and the superhuman feats of which humanity is capable when inspired by love, the most human of all feelings just because it mirrors the other love that gives humanity its ultimate meaning.

I agree that *Figaro* is Mozart's most perfect opera. Personally I consider it the greatest opera ever written. Nevertheless my personal favourite of the four great Mozart operas has always been *Così*. Of it, Mr Levin writes as follows:

Though it is absurd to call it immoral, [*Così*] does have a disturbing quality of cynicism .... Who loves cynicism? Well, cynics obviously; but they are, happily, few and the lovers of *Così fan tutte* many. True, it is musically the most perfectly constructed and worked out of the four operas, but of course it is much more than the music... It is an opera which requires a streak of pessimism in those who respond most fully to it. Pessimism, mind, not cycnism; the cynic rejoices in disaster, the pessimist merely expects it. Which leaves the cynic to tell the pessimists in the audience, over the protests of the two lovers, that fidelity among women is like that fabled bird, the phoenix — everyone has heard of it but no one has seen it!

* This broadcast was reprinted in *The Listener* in 1981.

If I may take gentle exception to this, I think that for once there is a slight but definite division of intent between da Ponte's text and Mozart's music. Da Ponte, as you might imagine, is a perfect cynic, but Mozart is not a perfect cynic, and he involves himself far more than the text warrants in the fates of the ladies when their roles are reversed. This is partly because Mozart always shows a special perception for the problems, aspirations and motivations of women, and partly because in order to convince the audience of the new state of affairs, he has not only provided the finest music for the most untruthful situations but almost seems at times to have persuaded himself to believe the lie.

Hence I believe that the particular poignancy of *Così fan tutte* is because the necessity for forgiveness — that omnipresent Mozartian grace — is present not only at the end of the opera but all through the scenes of deception, when we know — although the ladies do not yet — that their actions require more forgiveness than does any other action, perhaps, in any other Mozart opera. The emotions generated are therefore doubly powerful and the cynicism of the libretto is in part gainsaid.

John Hargreaves (Guglielmo), Peter Pears (Ferrando) and Owen Brannigan (Don Alfonso) with Sadler's Wells in 1944 (photo: Alexander Bender)

The Background to the Libretto

John Stone

In 1789 the poet Lorenzo da Ponte, already Mozart's librettist for *Figaro* and *Don Giovanni*, and at the time the dominant figure in Viennese operatic politics, offered the composer Antonio Salieri a new libretto. The piece was evidently a humorous commentary on da Ponte's relations with the soprano Adriana Ferrarese del Bene — who was to be the first Fiordiligi — and we find his friend Giacomo Casanova remarking in a letter shortly before the opera eventually came on: 'I laugh at the Ferrarese and the usual frankness of the poet. I believe he is most afflicted not to be able to appear on stage himself.'*

Salieri, who had become bitterly resentful of the ascendancy of da Ponte and his mistress, rejected the text as 'unworthy of musical invention' and it was subsequently offered to Mozart. Recent evidence from Mozart's autograph score, presented by Alan Tyson at a colloquium at King's College, London (1983), suggests the libretto was still undergoing radical transformation after Mozart commenced composition.

If there is any single underlying source for the plot it may perhaps be surprising to find it in a Chinese folktale which gained European currency in a Jesuit compilation, Duhalde's *Description de la Chine* (1735) — a standard reference work which also served Voltaire and Metastasio for material.† Set down by the then forgotten seventeenth-century scholar Feng-Meng Lung, it was adapted for Western audiences by the translator François-Xavier Dentrecolles.

The tale concerns the classical Taoist philosopher Chuang-Tse who plays a part analogous to that of the young officers in the opera. Chuang has been puzzled by a dream in which he is a huge butterfly flitting amongst the flowers of a garden, and he goes to visit Lao-Tse, the legendary founder of Taoism. Lao, our proto-type Don Alfonso, tells Chuang that his dream demonstrates the ephemeral nature of all passion.

Chuang retires from the world but marries a young woman called Tien. Failing to heed Lao's warning sufficiently, however, he begins, through his growing love for her, to form unrealistic expectations of her character.

One day an incident occurs which brings home to him the precarious nature of such dependence: he sees a young widow anxiously fanning the moist earth of her husband's grave. On enquiry he learns that she has sworn not to remarry until it is dry. Chuang summons up some spirits who perform the task on the instant and, accepting the fan as a thank-offering, goes on his way. At home Tien finds him brooding over it and he tells her his story.

She is so outraged by the account — for like Dorabella and Fiordiligi she protests her devotion too much — that she tears up the fan. Some days later

* This account is arrived at by careful consideration of *A Mozart Pilgrimage — The travel diaries of Vincent and Mary Novello in the year 1829*, ed. Nerina Medici and Rosemary Hughes, London 1955 and 1975 p. 127; da Ponte's memoirs passim; and *Carteggi Casanoviana* I p. 36 Palermo 1916.

† Voltaire's tragedy *L'Orphelin de la Chine* was based on a Chinese play printed in Duhalde. The folktale itself was also used by him in Chapter Two of *Zadig*. Metastasio cites as his sources for *L'Eroe Cinesi* based on an incident from Chinese history, 'Il Padre Du Halde ed altri' — in other words it is just the most familiar.

Jill Gomez (Fiordiligi) and Anna Reynolds (Dorabella) in the Scottish Opera production by Anthony Besch (photo: Bob Anderson)

Felicity Lott (Fiordiligi) and Della Jones (Dorabella) with the two 'deaths' on their hands, in the ENO production by John Cox (photo: Donald Southern)

Chuang dies — an event which, like the officers' embarkation for war, is not what it seems.

At the rites of mourning, observed during the hundred days preceding burial, Tien is approached by a young prince, who has only just arrived to study with Chuang. (He is of course an agent of Chuang — apparently a spirit in Feng's original, though his precise nature and identity remain obscure in Dentrecolles's translation). All too rapidly Tien conceives a violent passion for this stranger, and a precipitate wedding is arranged; though not before, in her eagerness, she has agreed to several dishonourable conditions.

As in the opera, the story is unravelled at an interrupted wedding feast. Paralleling the scene in Act One where the 'Albanians' pretend to take poison, the bridegroom falls desperately ill. His elderly servant then explains that the only remedy — certainly more gruesome than the magnet of Dr Mesmer produced by Despina — is the brain of a recently dead man mulled in wine. Equal to this new test, Tien breaks open Chuang's coffin with an axe — only to find that he has 'returned to life'.

Coming upon the scene of the suddenly-deserted feast, Chuang starts to reproach her. Before she can make any excuse he gives a sign and the prince and his servant reappear. Tien goes out and hangs herself. Chuang, with much ironic laughter, gives her a bizarre funeral, and, having burnt his house to the ground, leaves to spend his days in the company of his master Lao.

In the story great play is made of Chuang's laughter, a motif associated with the historical sage, and it re-emerges strongly in the opera. Don Alfonso's laughter is prominent all the way through, and he concludes with the advice: 'All four now laugh, as I have already laughed and will laugh'. The laughter is not of delight at the discomfiture of others, but that of philosophical detachment at the folly of human passion.

Dentrecolles's introduction to the tale seeks to mitigate its barbarous ending. He takes a somewhat loose approach to the original, smoothing over obscurities and carefully placing the story in the Epicurean tradition of worldly detachment to which the Jesuits approvingly likened Taoism. It is not the author's purpose, we are to understand, 'to weaken the unity . . . between married people' but to differentiate 'real and false merits' and demonstrate the danger of 'a love which is blind'. This is perhaps a recollection of the Epicurean poet, Lucretius (*De Rerum Natura* IV, 1153-4): 'Indeed men act for the most part blinded by passion and attribute qualities to women which are not properly theirs'. We are near to Don Alfonso's purpose too: the young officers should marry their girls, but not under the misapprehension that they are superhuman. Thus for all the discrepancy in tone several features in the opera seem to be specifically derived from the Chinese source, both in terms of the plot — the elderly philosopher, the woman who protests too much and the interrupted wedding feast — and of the explicit moral and philosophical outlook.

It is not merely the background of the eighteenth-century theatre: of the forms of Italian comic opera built from arias, recitatives, ensembles and extended finales; of the *commedia dell'arte* servant girl who deceives all those about her by assuming a series of disguises[1]; or of Marivaux's theatre of experiment, in which the laws of human behaviour are established under scientific conditions[2]. These are all things which are integral to the opera, but it has yet another ancestry. *Così fan tutte* brings together some of the central strands in European poetry.

Jean de la Fontaine remarks in his introduction to his *Contes et Nouvelles* (1669) — the collection of elegant verse tales in which the tradition of the

Sadler's Wells, 1963: Gerwyn Morgan (Guglielmo), Denis Dowling (Don Alfonso) and John Wakefield (Ferrando) (photo: Reg Wilson)

sexual anecdote reaches its literary apogee — that 'to condemn me is only to condemn Ariosto before me, and the ancients before Ariosto'. La Fontaine understands how stories become elaborated and merged, and defends the licence with which he continues the process — hoping, rather than otherwise, that people will recognise his models and appreciate the craftsmanship with which he has adapted them.

There is a great deal of this about *Così fan tutte*, and much in it has been absorbed from Ariosto's *Orlando Furioso* (1516), including the names of the female characters. In particular, two episodes — also pillaged by la Fontaine — have left their mark upon the opera. In one incident (Cantos XXVII and XXVIII), the Moorish king Rodomonte arrives at an inn and begins to quiz the assembled guests about the fidelity of their wives. Each insists that his is faithful until the inn-keeper takes a hand and, making Don Alfonso's familiar comparison of women's fidelity to the Arabian phoenix, tells a story whose symmetry puts one further in mind of the opera. This concerns two exceptionally handsome young men who discover their wives to be unfaithful and set off on a journey. Everywhere they go they find that all women are equally susceptible. Finally, wiser and more tolerant, they decide to return contentedly to their wives.[3]

The other relevant incident from *Orlando Furioso* belongs to a tradition which is more generally invoked in the opera — and indeed echoed by the Chinese story. It is the story of the man who, magically transformed, or in disguise, seduces his wife. The archetype for this is the tale of Cephalus and Procris from Book VII of Ovid's *Metamorphoses*[4]:

> The hunter Cephalus, newly married to Procris, is propositioned by the goddess Aurora and he refuses her. As he returns home meditating on

Ryszard Karczykowski (Ferrando), Thomas Allen (Guglielmo) and Donald Gramm (Don Alfonso) at Covent Garden in 1978 (photo: Christina Burton)

the capricious nature of womankind as personified by the goddess, his thoughts become infected with jealous suspicion of his wife, and he finds that by Aurora's agency his appearance has been transformed. In his new guise he approaches Procris and seduces her with offers of gifts. As she consents he resumes his old appearance and, horrified, she goes off to join Diana in the woods.

After a while they are reconciled and, as a peace offering, she presents him with a magic spear which will always hit its mark. Out hunting every day, Cephalus is in the habit of relaxing in remote, shady corners and calling on the breeze (Aura) to come and soothe his breast. Someone overhears him, and, thinking he is addressing a nymph, runs to tell Procris. The next day she goes to listen. Hearing a noise he hurls his spear and she is killed.

Cephalus's invocation to the breeze is deliberately echoed in *Così fan tutte* in Ferrando's *'Un'aura amorosa'*: 'A breeze of love from our beloved, a sweet restoration offers to the heart.' And in this case too there is a fatal ambiguity, since the specific identity of the beloved is dissolved in the all-pervading sweetness of the sentiment and the music.

In classical/medieval tradition the story becomes a double-edged moral homily on the corrosive nature of jealous suspicion and of avarice, and these two themes are closely reflected in Ariosto's version in Cantos XLII and XLIII of *Orlando Furioso*, which may be summarised as follows.

Outside Mantua one evening, Rinaldo is entertained by a mysterious knight who tells how, inflamed by jealous suspicion and transformed by a sorceress into the guise of one of his wife's former suitors, he had seduced her with offers of jewellery. In angry retribution she had gone off with the man whose

Sena Jurinac (Fiordiligi), Elena Rizzieri (Despina) and Nan Merriman (Dorabella) at Glyndebourne in 1956 (photo: Guy Gravett)

appearance he had assumed. The knight has challenged Rinaldo to drink from a magic goblet which possesses the property of spilling its contents over any cuckold. Sagely Rinaldo refuses the goblet in terms which are to be reiterated by Don Alfonso in the opera's opening trio:

> RINALDO 'Quite foolish would he be, who sought for what he did not wish to find.'
> DON ALFONSO 'O mad desire, to seek to uncover that evil, which found makes us wretched.'

But while Rinaldo here reproves the stupidity of gnawing doubt, Don Alfonso reproves that of reckless confidence. The continued form of Rinaldo's reply nevertheless points in the direction of the opera: he prefers to trust his wife, while recognising that like other women she is susceptible. Similarly, at the

38

end of *Così fan tutte* when the sisters promise that they will never in future be unfaithful, the two officers reply that they believe them but will not put it to the test.

The theme is further expanded in two subsequent versions of the story. Thus in la Fontaine's remodelling of Ariosto, *La Coupe Enchantée* (*The Magic Goblet*), the race of husbands are addressed to the effect that being a cuckold is a useful thing — people are kind to them — and Renaud (Rinaldo) by his judicious answer frees an army of husbands, tricked by the knight, from a curse: the principle of tolerance has come to dominate.

The final phase of transformation is to be found, however, in Christoph Martin Wieland's poem *Aurora und Cephalus* of 1768. Although we cannot be sure that Mozart knew it, it is at least a worthwhile speculation for of all German authors it was Wieland who was held in highest esteem by Mozart and his family. Indeed it was Wieland who edited the collection of fairy tales, *Djschinnistan*, which was to provide the stimulus for Mozart's masonic allegory, *Die Zauberflöte*, a year after *Così fan tutte*.

Wieland's verse tale, along with *Così fan tutte*, represents a tradition at its most self-conscious. It has overt allusions not only to Ovid but also to the reworkings of Ariosto and la Fontaine. In it the goddess Aurora sees in the youth Cephalus the image of her elderly husband Tithonus, as he was when he was young. (It was Tithonus, who was granted immortality but forgot to ask for eternal youth at the same time.) Cephalus is a young man of charm but exaggerated sensibility, as later Goethe's Werther and da Ponte's Ferrando were to be, and the element of jealous suspicion is just one aspect of his impressionability. When he tries to seduce Procris he appears first in the guise of a wealthy but ugly merchant, and then, anachronistically, as the handsome young lover Seladon from d'Urfé's *Astrée*. It is in this second role that he meets with success, so that the theme of avarice — of no great account in *Così fan tutte* — is explicitly rejected.

Following Ariosto, Procris goes off with the person whose appearance Cephalus has borrowed, and Cephalus tries to drown himself. He is saved by Aurora, and the poem closes with him sinking into her arms, and the poet lamenting that Boucher is not on hand to paint the scene. Interestingly the first edition of the poem was prefaced with a Latin motto which was considered so shocking that Wieland had to suppress it. It is a paraphrase of a line from Ovid's *Ars Amatoria* (Book II, 366) in which the gender has been changed from masculine to feminine: '— *quod faceret quaelibet, illa facit*' i.e. — what any woman would have done, she did'.[5]

The last text we must consider is the *Ars Amatoria* itself. Written in A.D.2 the poem scandalised the Emperor Augustus and was partially responsible for the poet's banishment from Rome some years later. Ovid used the conceit of an instruction manual in 'the art of love' to satirize the world of Roman sexual manners. The processes of seduction in *Così fan tutte* are conducted according to classical precedent. We begin with the approach to Despina:

> But first your intended female capture's maid to cultivate
> Take pains: she will make your access easy.
> Near to the counsels of her mistress should she be, see to it,
> But not too indiscreet in showing knowledge of your sport.
> Her you must promise, her corrupt with propositions:
> What you aim, with ease, if she so wills, you'll carry off.
>
> (*Ars Amatoria* I 351-6)

Hanneke Van Bork (Fiordiligi), Jane Berbié (Despina) and Anne Howells (Dorabella) in the 1969 Glyndebourne production (photo: Guy Gravett)

The ploy recommended in Ovid — since the victim is a married lady — is to choose a time when her husband has been unfaithful:

> Her in the morning the maid, combing her hair,
> Incites, and adding to the sail the work of oar,
> In sighing murmur, thinks out loud, and says:
> 'But, of course, you cannot pay him back in kind'.
> Then let her tell of you, then with persuasive arguments
> May she continue, and swear you die of insane love.
>
> (*Ars Amatoria* I 367-72)

The question of rivalry is at least hinted at in the opera when Despina, on learning of the departure of Ferrando and Guglielmo, suggests that it would be

Lois McDonall (Fiordiligi) and Sarah Walker (Dorabella) in the production for Sadler's Wells by Glen Byam Shaw (1974) (photo: Mike Humphrey)

best, 'to make love like murderesses, as your dear lovers will in camp'. Above all it is the psychological laws of Ovid's poem which seem to be invoked in the opera. Fiordiligi's anger is merely a facet of her emotional volatility, which can as easily turn to love. Ovid even anticipates the metaphor of her Act One aria:

> What is more hard than rock, more yielding than the wave?
> Penelope herself, only persist, with time you will vanquish ...
> ... Perhaps, and first, comes to you an angry letter,
> Which asks too, if you will, to cease vexatious protestations.
> What she asks, she fears; does not ask, longs for — that you insist:
> Continue, and soon will your desires gain fulfilment.
>
> (*Ars Amatoria* I 475-88)

A scene from the 1941 production by Nicola Benois designed by Ludwig Sievert at La Scala with Viorica Ursuleac and Eugenia Zareska as the sisters and Perisa Giri as Despina (Museo Teatrale alla Scala)

We also find foreshadowed the fate of Ferrando:

> It is to you to act the lover, affecting wounds by words:
> Belief in these of her you must acquire by any means ...
> ... Often though, he, who only by pretending starts, really loves;
> Often that, which formerly was feigned, becomes indeed.
>
> (*Ars Amatoria* I 611-8)

and finally the gall of Guglielmo when at the banquet his three friends join in their canon of forgetfulness:

> Alas, the treachery! Lovers should not fear their enemies:
> Those you believe faithful, flee, you will be safe.
> Of relative and brother beware, and your dearest friend:
> He truly will present to you such dreaded tribulation.
>
> (*Ars Amatoria* I 751-4)

*　　*　　*

The libretto of *Così fan tutte* has sometimes been represented as a typical opera text of its age. Eighteenth-century in character it certainly is, but it is also an artwork of unparalleled virtuosity, and its simple frame is a mask for the complexity of its content. It has its roots partly in da Ponte's cultural background as classical scholar and a professor of rhetoric, with Italy's poetic heritage in his veins. But this is not a sufficient explanation, because nothing else in his work approaches this level of creativity. Inevitably we turn towards Mozart.

Scenes from Anthony Besch's production for Scottish Opera designed by John Stoddart

Lilian Sukis (Fiordiligi) and Brigitte Fassbaender (Dorabella) at Covent Garden in 1979 (photo: Christina Burton)

Nemeček, his first biographer, wrote of him in 1798:

> Equally great was his talent for learning languages; he understood French, English, Italian and German. The Latin language he first learnt in later years, and that only to the extent as to understand church texts, that he might if the occasion required set them to music. In all the other languages he had read all the good authors and understood them.

Yet language was not Mozart's natural mode of expression, and he often also found that those words which were suitable for being set to music were not of the highest literary quality. That he absorbed the lessons of wide reading, however, seems evident. If we look at the way the natural imagery is employed in the text of *Così fan tutte* with a Shakespearean consistency and purposefulness we will not find a model for it among the general run of eighteenth-century librettos, nor even in da Ponte's. To find an exemplar we will have to go to Mozart's own *Idomeneo**.

In his memoirs da Ponte only referred to *Così fan tutte* in passing as 'the sister which holds third place among the daughters born of that most celebrated father of harmony'. He sounds content with the opera's Cinderella status, when he might have claimed it as his masterpiece. There is even an uncharacteristic suggestion that the work is essentially Mozart's property. But for all this, the game of allusion is played through to the end. Da Ponte has

---

* In *Ideomeneo* the metaphor is not thoroughly worked out in terms of drama; nevertheless it is more elaborate than any normally found in eighteenth-century opera. In Act One the storm in Elektra's head becomes the storm at sea which wrecks Idomeneo's fleet. In Act Two her softly melancholic emotions are at one with the placid sea.

Maria Ewing (Dorabella) and Bozena Betley (Fiordiligi) in Peter Hall's 1978 production at Glyndebourne (photo: Guy Gravett)

paraphrased the same lines from Ovid's *Tristia* (III xiv 13-18) which Mozart had used as the basis of his famous dedication of the *Haydn* string quartets, in which he commends his 'six children' to Haydn's guardianship.[6] The three children that Ovid refers to in writing to an 'unnamed friend' are the three books of the *Ars Amatoria*:

> Pallas-like, of me without a mother created
> Are my verses, this my family, my progeny is.
> This I commend to you, that the more bereft it is of parents,
> To you its guardian will the greater burden be.
> Three of my children are of my bad example followers;
> The others of the throng make openly to be your care.

Notes

[1] Alfred Einstein, *Mozart*, London 1971, p. 460.
[2] Charles Rosen, *The Classical Style*, London 1976, p. 314-5.
[3] See particularly Barbara Reynolds's translation of *Orlando Furioso*. Harmsworth 1977, vol. II, p. 172.
[4] In two articles in *The Warburg Journal* of 1954 Irving Lavin traced the tradition from Ovid to Ariosto. E.H. Gombrich added a post-script relating *Così fan tutte* to Book VII of *The Metamorphoses*. In *Da Ponte's Così fan tutte*, Göttingen 1973, Kurt Kramer picked up the threads of the journal and noted the textual correspondences in *Orlando Furioso* XLII and XLIII. Anne Livermore, *Music and Letters* 1965, argued that the opera derived from a play by Tirso de Molina, having failed to notice their common origin in Ovid.
[5] I am indebted to a commentary on the poem in *Perspectives and Points of View*, L.E. Kurth-Voigt, Baltimore and London 1974, p. 136-166.
[6] Mozart owned a copy of *Tristia* in parallel Latin/German text.

A playbill advertising the 1828 London performances of 'Tit for Tat', "altered and adapted from 'Così fan tutte'" (Royal Opera House Archives)

A Performance History

Nicholas John

The performance history of *Così* is perhaps more curious than of any other opera. Although Wagner even maintained that such an effete libretto could not inspire great music, and had not indeed done so, there have been many attempts to 'rescue' the music from the words. Countless versions were devised to modify the text for 19th-century morality; there were even productions where the music was married to wholly different stories.

The first German translation *Liebe und Versuchung* (*Love and Temptation*) by H.G. Schmieder and C.D. Stegmann was given in Frankfurt on May 1, 1791. Bretzner's version, *Weibertreue, oder Die Mädchen sind von Flandern* (*Women's Constancy, or The Girls from Flanders*), was first given in Leipzig in 1794. Renamed *The Two Aunts from Milan, or The Disguise*, this version was given in Vienna in 1802. His second version, this time divided into four acts, was entitled *The Wager or The Love and Artfulness of Women* and given in Stuttgart in 1796.

Of the many alternative German titles that followed during the century, G.F. Treitschke, one of Beethoven's librettists for *Fidelio*, made a standard version, *Mädchentreue* (*The Fidelity of Girls*), later entitled *Die Zauberprobe* (*The Magic Test*). In Weimar, 1830, the opera was presented as *Die Weiberkenner oder Wer hat die Wette gewonnen?* (*The Experts in Women or Who won the Wager?*). J.D. Anton's translation entitled *Die Guerillas* (*The Guerillas*) was given in Mayence in 1838. The singer Karl Scheidemantel made an attempt in 1909 to replace the libretto with one based on Calderón (*Die Dame Kobold — The Imp Woman*).

In Italy, the opera was given in Italian (Trieste 1797, Milan 1807, Turin 1814) generally as *La Scuola degli Amanti*, and it was also first heard in Paris in Italian (1813). A French libretto, *Le Laboureur Chinois*, was set to Berton's arrangement of extracts from *Così* and other works by Mozart, Haydn and Mayr in 1813. Later in the century, Barbier and Carré based a text on *Love's Labour's Lost* (*Peines d'Amour perdues*) for the 1869 production at the Théâtre Lyrique. Paris heard the original text in 1920 in a translation by Durdilly and Chantavoine, at the Opéra Comique (April 20).

London first heard the opera in Italian at the King's Theatre on May 9, 1811. *Tit for Tat; or The Tables Turned* was a translation done for an arrangement of the music by W. Hawes in 1828. In 1841, there were amateur performances as *The Retaliation*.

The translation made by the Reverend Marmaduke E. Browne for the students of the Royal College of Music on July 16, 1890 is the basis of the text printed here. It has been revised by many, including E.J. Dent for Lilian Baylis's English Opera Company at the Old Vic and Sadler's Wells.

And so to New York, where the first performances were given at the Met. in 1922 (March 24) in Italian.

Margaret Price as Fiordiligi at Covent Garden in 1978 (photo: Christina Burton)

Thematic Guide

Many of the themes from the opera have been identified in the articles by
numbers in square brackets, which refer to the themes set out on these pages.
The themes are also identified by the numbers in brackets at the corresponding
points in the libretto, so that the words can be related to the musical themes.

[1] FERRANDO
Allegro

Sus-pect Do - ra - bel - la? The is ab-surd, the is ab - surd!
thought thought
La mia Do - ra - bel-la ca-pa-ce non è, ca-pa-ce non è;

[2] DON ALFONSO
Allegro scherzando

Wo-man's faith is like the phoe-nix in re - mote A - ra - bia dwell-ing,
E la fe - de del-le fem-mi-ne co-me l'a - ra-ba fe - ni - ce;

[3] FIORDILIGI
Andante dolce

This por-trait a - lone is the face of A - don-is,
Ah, guar-da, so - rel-la, ah, guar-da, so - rel-la,

[4] *Maestoso*

[5] DORABELLA
Allegro agitato

Cease not, re - morse-less love, thus to tor - ment me,
Sma - nie im - pla - ca - bi-li, che m'a-gi - ta - te,

[6] DESPINA
Allegretto

For in re - al - i - ty, void of de-vo - tion, Leaves e-ver flutt'-ring,
Di pa-sta si - mi-le son tut-ti quan-ti, son tut-ti quan-ti:

49

[7] GUGLIELMO

O vi - sion so charm-ing, Your an - ger dis - arm - ing,
Non sia - te ri - tro - si Oc - chiet - ti vez - zo - si,

[8] FERRANDO

From eyes so al - lur - ing Our hope re - as - sur - ing
Un' au - ra a - mo - ro - sa Del no - stro te - so - ro

[9] DESPINA
Andante

At fif - teen a girl al - rea - dy Must be tru - ly wise and world - ly,
U - na don-na a quin-di-ci an-ni Dee sà - per... o - gni gran mo - da;

[10] DORABELLA
Andante

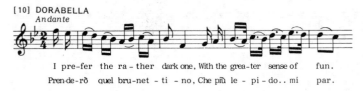

I pre - fer the ra - ther dark one, With the grea - ter sense of fun.
Pren-de-rò quel bru-net - ti - no, Che più le - pi - do.. mi par.

[11] GUGLIELMO
Andante grazioso

This heart that I give thee, I pray you to trea - sure,
Il co - re vi do - no, Bell' i - do - lo mi - o!

[12] FIORDILIGI
Adagio

Ah, my love, I pray for-give-ness For the wrong my soul has har-boured
Per pie - tà, ben mio, per - do - na All' er - ror d'un al - ma a-man-te;

[13] GUGLIELMO
Allegretto

La-dies have such var-i - a-tions, Permu-ta-tions, compli - ca - tions!
Donne mie, la fa-te a tanti È tan-ti, a tan-ti e tan-ti, a tan - ti!

50

FERRANDO
Allegro

Her trea-son is poi-son that tor - tures my heart,
Tra - di - to, scher-ni -to dal per - fi - do cor,

[15] **DORABELLA**
Allegretto vivace

Young Love is un - re - lent - ing, A ser-pent full of wiles,
È l'A - mo - re un la - dron-cel - lo, Un ser-pent-el - lo è A - mor,

[16] **FIORDILIGI**
Adagio

All too slow-ly the hours are fleet-ing,
Fra gli am-ple - ssi, in po-chi i-stan-ti,

[17] **DESPINA**
Allegro assai

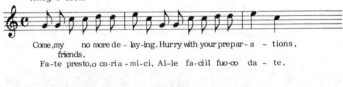

Come, my no more de - lay-ing. Hurry with your prepar-a - tions,
friends,
Fa - te presto, o ca-ri a - mi-ci, Al-le fa-ci il fuo-co da - te,

[18] *Andante*

Now may love, that has u - ni - ted With de-light be-yond ex-press-ing,
Be - ne - det - ti i dop-pi coniugi, E le a - ma-bi - li spo-si - ne,

Above: Aix-en-Provence, 1965: left to right, Michel Sénéchal, Teresa Stich-Randall, Teresa Berganza, Dino Mantovani (photo: Serge Lido). Below left: Salzburg, 1969: Anneliese Rothenberger, Rosalind Elias, Lajos Kozma, Tom Krause, Walter Berry. Below right: Dietrich Fischer-Dieskau (top), Hermann Prey (left), Peter Schreier (right), Gundula Janowitz (left), Brigitte Fassbaender (right). (P.S.F.)

Above: Aix-en-Provence, 1977: Francisco Araiza, Gabriel Bacquier, Knut Scram. Below: 1980: Francisco Araiza, Valerie Masterson, Sylvia Lindenstrand, Knut Scram (photos: Bernand).

The mesmeric cure at Glyndebourne, 1978, in Peter Hall's production designed by John Bury (photo: Guy Gravett)

A little later in the same scene at ENO, 1981, in John Cox's production designed by Roger Butlin (photo: Catherine Ashmore)

Così fan tutte

o sia La Scuola degli amanti
(or The School for Lovers)

Dramma Giacoso in Two Acts
by Wolfgang Amadeus Mozart

Libretto by Lorenzo da Ponte

English version by the Reverend Marmaduke E. Browne
revised by John Cox

Così fan tutte was first performed at the Burgtheater, Vienna, on January 26, 1790. The first performance in England was at the King's Theatre in the Haymarket, London on May 9, 1811. The first performance in America was on March 24, 1922 at the Metropolitan Opera.

Note on the various versions of 'Così fan tutte'

Although the opera was given in other cities during Mozart's lifetime — Prague, Dresden and Frankfurt-am-Main — the composer had nothing to do with these performances, nor, apparently, with the German staging in Munich for which he was, wrongly, reputed to have made some adaptations. There is only the one series of performances at the Burgtheater in Vienna with which Mozart was connected, and the first few evenings of which he conducted himself. But in the course of the rehearsals, at which Haydn was twice present, Mozart cancelled a brilliant and large-scale aria, *'Rivolgete a lui lo sguardo'* (K. 584) (see p. 124), composed for Benucci and entered as a separate item in Mozart's own thematic catalogue. Apparently Mozart and da Ponte decided that this aria would occupy too dominant a position in Act Two and replaced it with No. 15, *'Non siate ritrosi'*. The original aria, which is for a large orchestra (oboes, bassoons, trumpets, timpani and also, at first, horns, which Mozart later cancelled), is often given as a concert piece. Mozart also made some cuts in his own autograph, not all of them really necessary or advisable (Einstein called them 'heartless'). The autograph from the former Prussian State Library in Berlin is one of those placed in Grüssau Monastery (now in Poland) during World War Two and recently recovered by the Polish authorities.

* * *

This Italian text is based on the edition made by Paolo Lecaldano for Rizzoli (*Tre Libretti per Mozart*, Milan, 1956). There da Ponte's autograph version is presented with carefully systematised stage-directions, modernised and consistent spellings, and regular punctuation. His aim was to produce an accurate version of the literary text. We have varied from this where the text differs from what Mozart finally set to music. While the layout and stage-directions follow the original libretto as far as possible, we have reverted to certain archaisms of spelling and inserted Mozart's words in order to present what is actually sung. The stage-directions have very occasionally been supplemented by those in the score, where there is no indication at all in the libretto. As such they represent no actual production and do not form part of the Browne/Cox version.

Translator's Note

The English version of *Così fan tutte* which provides the basis for that used in this production was, according to the title page of the Novello score, 'translated and adapted from the original Italian and from the German paraphrase, by the Rev. Marmaduke E. Browne', and 'was first performed by pupils of the Royal College of Music, at the Savoy Theatre, London, July 16, 1890; conductor, Professor C.V. Stanford'.

We chose it from those available for its deft and fluent versification, its delicate lyricism and its urbanity. Nevertheless, it was the work of a man of the cloth, writing in the last century and for students. These facts, combined with the opera's reputation for moral turpitude, led Browne in several instances a long way from da Ponte's original text. Fiordiligi and Guglielmo were renamed Isadora and Gratiano. But it was the character of Despina that suffered most as a result. The mildest social criticism was suppressed, for example, and her frequent references to the devil were not translated. All the women were attributed with no more sexual awareness than a vague romantic ardour. This distorted the wider moral implications of the text, which worried and displeased so many 19th-century commentators.

This adaption was initially made for my production in 1980 by English National Opera at the London Coliseum. It has been revised for publication since this complete edition of the libretto includes several passages cut even in the exceptionally full version which was performed. The purpose has been to produce a version retaining the best of Marmaduke Browne, while bringing the whole as near as possible to da Ponte. — John Cox

Photographs by Alexander Bender of the two casts in the 1944 Sadler's Wells production: left, Joan Cross and Peter Pears, and right, Marion Lowe and Richard Lewis

CHARACTERS

Fiordiligi ⎫ *sisters from Ferrara*   *soprano*
Dorabella ⎭ *dwelling in Naples*   *mezzo-soprano*
Guglielmo *Fiordiligi's lover* ⎫ *officers*   *tenor*
Ferrando *Dorabella's lover* ⎭   *baritone*
Despina *a chamber maid*   *soprano*
Don Alfonso *an old philosopher*   *bass*
Chorus of Soldiers and People
Chorus of Sailors
Chorus of Servants

The action is set in Naples.

Felicity Lott (Fiordiligi) and Della Jones (Dorabella) in the 1981 ENO production by John Cox (photo: Donald Southern)

58

Act One

Scene One. *A coffee shop. Ferrando, Don Alfonso and Guglielmo. / No. 1 Terzetto*

FERRANDO

Suspect Dorabella?
The thought is absurd!
No power could compel her
To forfeit her word.

[1] La mia Dorabella
Capace non è:
Fedel quanto bella
Il cielo la fe'.

GUGLIELMO

Suspect Fiordiligi,
She's honest as day,
The one who adores her
She ne'er would betray.

La mia Fiordiligi
Tradirmi non sa:
Uguale in lei credo
Costanza e beltà.

DON ALFONSO

My temples are greying,
I speak from experience.
So argue no longer,
I've finished my say.

Ho i crini già grigi,
Ex cathedra parlo;
Ma tali litigi
Finiscano qua.

FERRANDO AND GUGLIELMO

No! No! You have spoken
Of vows to be broken,
Produce us some token
That such is the case.

No, detto ci avete
Che infide esser ponno:
Provar ce 'l dovete,
Se avete onestà.

DON ALFONSO

I don't understand you.

Tai prove lasciamo ...

FERRANDO AND GUGLIELMO
(putting their hands on their swords)

Say on, we comand you,
Or else we will brand you
A coward and base.

No, no, le vogliamo:
O, fuori la spada,
Rompiam l'amistà.

DON ALFONSO
(aside)

O foolish devotion!
'Twill end but in sadness
To seek to discover
The thorn on a rose.

O pazzo desire!
Cercar di scoprire
Quel mal che, trovato,
Meschini ci fa.

FERRANDO AND GUGLIELMO
(aside)

Whoe'er has the courage
Her truth to disparage,
Will find in her lover
The direst of foes.

Sul vivo mi tocca
Chi lascia di bocca
Sortire un accento
Che torto le fa.

Secco Recitative

Swords or pistols? For
Both of us demand satisfaction.

Fuor la spada! Scegliete
Qual di noi più vi piace.

DON ALFONSO
(calmly)

I'm a peaceable person
And I handle no steel except at table.

Io son uomo di pace,
E duelli non fo, se non a mensa.

FERRANDO

You'll have to fight, or declare at once	O battervi, o dir subito
The reason for your vile insinuation.	Perchè d'infedeltà le nostre amanti
Your suspicion is treason!	Sospettate capaci!

DON ALFONSO

Credulity of youth, how you amuse me!	Cara semplicità, quanto mi piaci!

FERRANDO

You cynical old rogue, I swear by heaven! ...	Cessate di scherzar, o giuro al cielo! ...

DON ALFONSO

And I swear by experience,	Ed io, giuro alla terra,
For this time I'm not joking.	Non scherzo, amici miei.
I only want to know	Solo saper vorrei
What special type of being	Che razza d'animali
You've managed to discover.	Son queste vostre belle,
Have they, like the rest of us,	Se han come tutti noi carne,
feelings, thoughts and emotions?	ossa e pelle,
Are these two creatures goddesses,	Se mangian come noi, se veston gonne?
Or are they women, no more, no less?	Alfin, se Dee, se donne son ...

FERRANDO AND GUGLIELMO

They're women;	Son donne,
But ... perfection ... perfection ...	Ma ... son tali ... son tali ...

DON ALFONSO

The truly faithful woman	E in donne pretendete
You believe can exist?	Di trovar fedeltà?
Such simple trust as yours I can't resist.	Quanto mi piaci mai, semplicità!

No. 2 Terzetto
(jokingly)

Woman's faith is like the phoenix	[2]	È la fede delle femmine
In remote Arabia dwelling.		Come l'araba fenice;
Travellers such tales are telling;		Che vi sia, ciascun lo dice;
Have they seen it? No, no, not they.		Dove sia, nessun lo sa.

FERRANDO
(eagerly)

Such a one is Dorabella!	La fenice è Dorabella!

GUGLIELMO
(eagerly)

Such a one is Fiordiligi!	La fenice è Fiordiligi!

DON ALFONSO

Boasting empty as a bubble:	Non è questa, non è quella:
Women true? They never were.	Non fu mai, non vi sarà.

Secco Recitative

FERRANDO

A poetical fiction!	Scioccherie di poeti!

GUGLIELMO

Eternal sneer of cynics!	Scempiaggini di vecchi!

DON ALFONSO

So be it, but listen.	Orbene, udite,
Don't take offence so readily,	Ma senza andar in collera:
What proof have you yet found that these dear creatures	Qual prova avete voi che ognor costanti
Have such unusual natures;	Vi sien le vostre amanti;
That to you they are bound by a link that no friction	Chi vi fe' sicurtà che invariabili

Can sever?   Sono i lor cori?

FERRANDO

     Personal acquaintance ...   Lunga esperienza ...

GUGLIELMO

Fine education ...   Nobil educazion ...

FERRANDO

     Of kindred feeling ...   Pensar sublime ...

GUGLIELMO

No thought of self at all ...   Analogia d'umor ...

FERRANDO

     Nothing concealing ...   Disinteresse ...

GUGLIELMO

Sympathetic and affable!   Immutabil carattere ...

FERRANDO

     Engagement ...   Promesse ...

GUGLIELMO

Betrothal ...   Proteste ...

FERRANDO

     Protestations ...   Giuramenti ...

DON ALFONSO

Blushes, and sighs, embraces, palpitations,   Pianti, sospir, carezze, svenimenti.
Forgive me if I laugh at you.   Lasciatemi un po' ridere ...

FERRANDO

     Confound it!   Cospetto!
What have we said that's laughable? Finite di deriderci?

DON ALFONSO

     Excuse me!   Pian piano;
What if I give you proof you   E se toccar con mano
Cannot deny, they're just like other Oggi vi fo che come l'altre sono?
   women?

GUGLIELMO

Folly to try!   Non si può dar!

FERRANDO

  Absurd!   Non è!

DON ALFONSO

    A bet?   Giochiam!

FERRANDO

   We'll bet you!   Giochiamo!

DON ALFONSO

A hundred guineas.   Cento zecchini.

GUGLIELMO

  A thousand if you'd rather.   E mille, se volete.

DON ALFONSO

You'll take it?   Parola ...

61

FERRANDO

Here's my hand on it.   Parolissima.

DON ALFONSO

Remember, no whispers, no hinting   E un cenno, un motto, un gesto
To your Penelopes that we are thinking   Giurate di non far di tutto questo
Of having sport without their knowing.   Alle vostre Penelopi.

FERRANDO

We swear it –   Giuriamo.

DON ALFONSO

On the word of a soldier.   Da soldati d'onore.

GUGLIELMO

On the word of a soldier.   Da soldati d'onore.

DON ALFONSO

You swear the task I set you   E tutto quel farete
Boldly to carry through.   Ch'io vi dirò di far.

FERRANDO

Try us!   Tutto!

GUGLIELMO

Try anything.   Tuttissimo!

DON ALFONSO

Bravissimi!   Bravissimi!

FERRANDO AND GUGLIELMO

Bravissimo,   Bravissimo,
Signor Don Alfonsetto!   Signor Don Alfonsetto!

FERRANDO

        And when we've won it,   A spese vostre
See if you find that funny.   Or ci divertiremo.

GUGLIELMO
(to Ferrando)

Have you thought of a way to spend your   E de' cento zecchini, che faremo?
money?

No. 3 Terzetto

FERRANDO

I shall hire a band of players   Una bella serenata
And a serenade I'll bring her.   Far io voglio alla mia Dea.
Drums and trumpets   Far io voglio,
Shall accompany the singer.   Far io voglio alla mia Dea.

GUGLIELMO

I've a better gift to offer   In onor di Citerea
Than your music and your song.   Un convito io voglio far.
I shall give a lavish party   In onor di Citerea
And we'll revel loud and long.   Un convito io voglio far.

DON ALFONSO

May I have an invitation?   Sarò anch'io de' convitati?

FERRANDO AND GUGLIELMO

Yes, of course sir, that you may   Ci sarete, si signor.
For you'll have the bill to pay.   Ci sarete, si signor.

| And with love and wine united | E che brindis replicati |
| Swift shall pass the hours away. | Far vogliamo al Dio d'amor! |

(They depart.)

Scene Two. *A garden by the seashore. Fiordiligi and Dorabella. The two girls are each looking at a miniature hanging at their waists. / No. 4 Duet*

FIORDILIGI

This portrait alone is	[3]	Ah, guarda, sorella,
The face of Adonis		Se bocca più bella,
But nought to the image		Se aspetto più nobile
Enshrined in my heart.		Si può ritrovar.

DORABELLA

Ah, then it must follow,	Osserva tu un poco
That this is Apollo!	Che fuoco ha ne' sguardi!
But tenfold more lovely	Se fiamma, se dardi
In nature than art!	Non sembran scoccar.

FIORDILIGI

| No aspect is wanting; | Si vede un sembiante |
| A warrior and a lover! | Guerriero ed amante. |

DORABELLA

| You see here a feature | Si vede una faccia |
| So gentle and relentless. | Che alletta e minaccia. |

FIORDILIGI AND DORABELLA

| I'm feeling so happy! | Io sono felice! |

If other delight me	Se questo mio core,
Let Cupid requite me:-	Mai cangia desio,
May Fortune implant in my bosom	Amore mi faccia
The pain of his dart.	Vivendo penar!

Secco Recitative

FIORDILIGI

I can't think what's the matter –	Mi par che stamattina volentieri
I've a silly desire for an adventure, a little mischief.	Farei la pazzarella: ho un certo fuoco,
There's something in my veins that makes me tingle.	Un certo pizzicor entro le vene ...
When Guglielmo gets here, just to tease him,	Quando Guglielmo viene, se sapessi
I'll ask him what it means.	Che burla gli vo' far.

DORABELLA

Would you believe it?	Per dirti il vero,
I awoke today humming	Qualche cosa di nuovo
A tune that will not leave me, it does not falter,	Anch'io nell'alma provo: io giurerei
I believe it's to do with Hymen's altar.	Che lontane non siam dagli imenei.

FIORDILIGI

Give me your hand then, and let me tell your fortune:	Dammi la mano, io voglio astrologarti.
Oh, what a life-line, look where	Uh, che bell'*Emme*! E questo
It goes, it must mean you'll soon be married.	È un *Pi*! Va bene: *m*atrimonio *p*resto.

DORABELLA

| D'you think I would resist it? | Affè, che ci avrei gusto! |

FIORDILIGI

| I wouldn't be against it. | Ed io non ci avrei rabbia. |

But it seems that the men who are in prospect	Ma che diavol vuol dir che i nostri sposi
Don't mean to come today? How disappointing.	Ritardano a venir? Son già le sei ...

FIORDILIGI

Here they are.	Eccoli.

Scene Three. *Fiordiligi, Dorabella and Don Alfonso.*

DORABELLA

You're mistaken, it's their companion, Don Alfonso.	Non son essi: è Don Alfonso, L'amico lor.

FIORDILIGI

So happy To see Don Alfonso.	Ben venga Il signor Don Alfonso!

DON ALFONSO

Dearest ladies.	Riverisco.

DORABELLA

What now? Where are the others? You are sighing.	Cos'è? perchè qui solo? Voi piangete?
Your news? For goodness sake, quick let us hear it!	Parlate, per pietà: che cosà è nato?
Ferrando!	D'amante ...

FIORDILIGI

Guglielmo.	L'idol mio ...

DON ALFONSO

How will you bear it?	Barbaro fato!

No. 5 Aria

Let me try. My courage fails	Vorrei dir, e cor non ho,
To deliver the dreadful news;	Balbettando il labbro va;
At the task my spirit quails,	Fuor la voce uscir non può,
Words forsake me, lips refuse.	Ma mi resta mezza qua.
What to counsel? What to do?	Che farete? che farò?
How to meet the cruel blow!	Oh, che gran fatalità!
As I weep for them, for you,	Dar di peggio non si può:
How to say I do not know.	Ho di voi, di lor pietà!

Secco Recitative

FIORDILIGI

Tell us, for pity's sake, Signor Alfonso,	Stelle! Per carità, signor Alfonso,
Do not torture us so.	Non ci fate morir.

DON ALFONSO

My dear young ladies, You will need all your courage.	Convien armarvi, Figlie mie, di costanza.

DORABELLA

Oh Heaven!	O Dei! Qual male
What awful thing has come to pass. What can have happened?	É addivenuto mai, qual caso rio?
Can my lover be injured?	Forse è morto il mio bene?

FIORDILIGI

Can mine be dying?	È morto il mio?

DON ALFONSO

Dead . . . they are not; with death the worst is over!

Morti . . . non son; ma poco men che morti.

DORABELLA

The smallpox?

Feriti?

DON ALFONSO

No.

No.

FIORDILIGI

Or the gangrene?

Ammalati?

DON ALFONSO

Not yet.

Neppur.

FIORDILIGI

Do tell us plainly.

Che cosa, dunque?

DON ALFONSO

For active service
They are both under orders.

Al marzial campo
Ordin regio li chiama.

FIORDILIGI AND DORABELLA

Oh God! How awful!

Ohimè, che sento!

FIORDILIGI

When must they leave?

E partiran?

DON ALFONSO

This morning.

Sul fatto.

DORABELLA

And is there
Nothing can exempt them?

E non v'è modo
D'impedirlo?

DON ALFONSO

Oh, no!

Non v'è.

FIORDILIGI

Shall we not see them?

Nè un solo addio? . . .

DON ALFONSO

In their sorrow they had not
The courage to demand it.
But if you would receive them,
They're ready.

Gli infelici non hanno
Coraggio di vedervi.
Ma se voi lo bramate,
Son pronti . . .

DORABELLA

Are they here?

Dove son?

DON ALFONSO

I've told them. Come forward.

Amici, entrate.

Scene Four. *Fiordiligi, Dorabella, Don Alfonso; Ferrando and Guglielmo in travelling clothes. / No. 6 Quintet*

GUGLIELMO

Courage fails me! For no evasion
Can the dreadful truth dissemble.

Sento, oddio, che questo piede
È restio nel girle avante.

FERRANDO

In my anguish, how I tremble,
As I inform you we must part.

Il mio labbro palpitante
Non può detto pronunziar.

DON ALFONSO

In the face of such calamity	Nei momenti i più terribili
Then the hero's courage rises!	Sua virtù l'eroe palesa.

FIORDILIGI AND DORABELLA

Spare us other dread surprises!	Or che abbiam la nuova intesa,
If the worst be yet unspoken,	A voi resta a fare il meno.
Ere the awful news be broken,	Fate core: a entrambe in seno
Plunge a dagger in my heart.	Immergeteci l'acciar.

FERRANDO AND GUGLIELMO

My beloved, it's fate ordaining,	Idol mio, la sorte incolpa,
Cruel fate, that cries 'depart'.	Se ti deggio abbandonar.

DORABELLA

Ah, no, no, you shall not leave me.	Ah, no, no, non partirai!

FIORDILIGI

Love can conquer fate, believe me!	No, crudel, non te ne andrai!

DORABELLA

I will die, my life disdaining.	Voglio pria cavarmi il core!

FIORDILIGI

You are mine while life's remaining.	Pria ti vo' morire ai piedi!

FERRANDO
(aside to Don Alfonso)

There you see now!	Cosa dici?

GUGLIELMO
(aside to Don Alfonso)

As we told you!	Te n'avvedi?

DON ALFONSO
(aside to the two men)

To your bargain still I hold you!	Saldo, amico: *finem lauda.*

FIORDILIGI, DORABELLA, FERRANDO, GUGLIELMO AND DON ALFONSO

Ah! While fate is thus designing,	Il destin così defrauda
Ever pain with joy combining,	Le speranze de' mortali.
Human pleasure undermining,	Ah, chi mai fra tanti mali,
Nought to life can bliss impart.	Chi mai può la vita amar?

*Secco Recitative**

GUGLIELMO

Ah! Do not weep, my love!	Non piangere, idol mio!

FERRANDO

My heart's adored one,		Non disperarti,
Let not grief thus o'erwhelm you.	Adorata mia sposa!	

DON ALFONSO

No, leave them yet that solace,	Lasciate lor tal sfogo: è troppo
for this, their anguish,	giusta
They have cause all-sufficing.	La cagion di quel pianto.

(The lovers embrace tenderly.)

FIORDILIGI

Again I'll never see you!	Chi sa s'io più ti veggio!

---

* This recitative and duettino are often cut in performance.

DORABELLA

No more my own to call you!　　　　　Chi sa se più ritorni!

FIORDILIGI

Take now, I pray, your dagger,　　　　Lasciami questo ferro: ei mi dia
　and end this life,　　　　　　　　　　morte,
Henceforth lonely and dreary,　　　　Se mai barbara sorte
Let me die on your bosom!　　　　　　In quel seno a me caro ...

DORABELLA

I die of sorrow, keener than any　　　Morrei di duol; d'uopo non ho
　dagger.　　　　　　　　　　　　　d'acciaro.

FERRANDO AND GUGLIELMO

Oh, leave that vow unspoken,　　　　Non farmi, anima mia,
Do not part from me weeping,　　　　Questi infausti presagi.
Be this last kiss the token,　　　　　Proteggeran gli Dei
Till my return you'll rest in Heaven's　La pace del tuo cor ne' giorni
keeping.　　　　　　　　　　　　　miei.

No. 7 Duettino

The stern call of duty　　　　　　　Al fato dan legge
With brave heart obeying,　　　　　Quegli occhi vezzosi:
Sweet visions of beauty　　　　　　Amor li protegge,
Our anguish allaying,　　　　　　　Nè i loro riposi
Be angels to guard as　　　　　　　Le barbare stelle
We march on our way.　　　　　　　Ardiscon turbar.

Till quickly returning　　　　　　　Il ciglio sereno,
We banish your mourning,　　　　　Mio bene, a me gira:
And laughter shall scatter　　　　　Felice al tuo seno
The tears of today.　　　　　　　　Io spero tornar.

Secco Recitative

DON ALFONSO
(aside)

What a talent for acting! So true to nature,　La commedia è graziosa, e tutti e due
And capitally spoken.　　　　　　　Fan ben la loro parte.

(A drum sounds in the distance.)

FERRANDO

　　　　That signal!　　　　　　　O cielo! questo
The drum pronounces our sentence.　È il tamburo funesto
Can I leave you, those tender arms denying!　Che a divider mi vien dal mio tesoro.

DON ALFONSO

See the boat is arriving!　　　　　　Ecco, amici, la barca.

FIORDILIGI

　　　I'm fainting!　　　　　　　　Io manco.

DORABELLA

　　　I'm dying!　　　　　　　　　Io moro.

Scene Five. *Fiordiligi, Dorabella, Don Alfonso, Ferrando, Guglielmo, soldiers and people.*
A military march in the distance. A boat arrives at the shore; then a troop of soldiers enters,
accompanied by a crowd of townspeople. / No. 8 Chorus [4]

CHORUS
(soldiers and people)

Oh, the soldier's life for me!　　　　Bella vita militar!
Ever o'er new countries ranging,　　Ogni di si cangia loco,
Daily scene and fortune changing,　Oggi molto, doman poco,
Now on land, and now on sea.　　　Ora in terra ed or sul mar.

Overhead the trumpet sounding,	Il fragor di trombe e pifferi,
In his heart high courage bounding,	Lo sparar di schioppi e bombe
Comrades brave and faithful surrounding,	Forza accresce al braccio e all'anima,
That the soldier's life should be.	Vaga sol di trionfar.
Oh, the soldier's life for me!	Bella vita militar!

Secco Recitative

DON ALFONSO

My friends, the time is flying, tarry no longer:	Non v'è più tempo, amici: andar conviene
For you must go where duty alone invites you.	Ove il destino, anzi il dover v'invita.

FIORDILIGI

My life!	Mio cor . . .

DORABELLA

My best beloved!	Idolo mio . . .

FERRANDO

My love!	Mio ben . . .

GUGLIELMO

My darling!	Mia vita . . .

FIORDILIGI

Give me one look to treasure.	Ah, per un sol momento . . .

DON ALFONSO

I see the last detachment	Del vostro reggimento
Has embarked on the galley;	Già è partita la barca.
To take the tardy few like you who linger	Raggiungerla convien coi pochi amici
There's a boat getting ready,	Che su legno più lieve
And awaiting your signal.	Attendendo vi stanno.

FERRANDO AND GUGLIELMO

One last embrace, beloved.	Abbracciami, idol mio!

FIORDILIGI AND DORABELLA

Death would be easier.	Muoio d'affanno.

No. 9 Quintet

FIORDILIGI
(*weeping*)

You'll write long letters often,	Di scrivermi ogni giorno
The cruel blow to soften.	Giurami, vita mia!

DORABELLA
(*weeping*)

No less than two a day,	Due volte ancora
My dearest, you promise.	Tu scrivimi, se puoi.

FERRANDO

A sweet task you set me!	Sii certa, o cara.

GUGLIELMO

Oh, yes, doubt not my complying.	Non dubitar, mio bene.

DON ALFONSO
(*aside*)

I'll crease myself with laughter.	Io crepo, se non rido!

FIORDILIGI

Think of me night and day!	Sii costante a me sol . . .

DORABELLA

Never betray me!   Serbati fido.

FERRANDO

Farewell!   Addio!

GUGLIELMO

Farewell!   Addio!

FIORDILIGI AND DORABELLA, FERRANDO AND GUGLIELMO

What torture racks my heart,   Mi si divide il cor, bell'idol
  no words can tell.   mio!
Farewell, love, farewell!   Addio, addio, addio!

DON ALFONSO
(*aside*)

I'll crease myself with laughter.   Io crepo, se non rido!

CHORUS

Oh, the soldier's life for me!   [4]   Bella vita militar!
Ever o'er new countries ranging,   Ogni dì si cangia loco,
Daily scene and fortune changing,   Oggi molto, doman poco,
Now on land, and now on sea.   Ora in terra ed or sul mar.

Overhead the trumpet sounding,   Il fragor di trombe e pifferi,
In his heart high courage bounding,   Lo sparar di schioppi e bombe
Comrades brave and faithful   Forza accresce al braccio e
  surrounding,   all'anima,
That the soldier's life should be.   Vaga sol di trionfar.

Oh, the soldier's life for me!   Bella vita militar!

(*While the chorus is repeated, Ferrando and Guglielmo get into the boat, which then disappears into the distance amidst the sound of drums, etc.. The soldiers leave, followed by the townspeople. The sisters remain as if transfixed on the sea shore.*)

Scene Six. *Fiordiligi, Dorabella and Don Alfonso. / Secco Recitative*

DORABELLA
(*as if waking from a trance*)

Are they gone?   Dove son?

DON ALFONSO

They have left us.   Son partiti.

FIORDILIGI

    Ah, why has fortune   Oh, dipartenza
So untimely bereft us?   Crudelissima! amara!

DON ALFONSO

    Be courageous,   Fate core,
Call hope to your assistance.   Carissime figliuole.
    (*A kerchief is seen waving in the distance.*)
For see there in the distance   Guardate, da lontano
Still with waving of kerchiefs they caress   Vi fan cenno con mano i cari sposi.
  you.

FIORDILIGI
(*waving*)

God bless you, my darling!   Buon viaggio, mia vita!

DORABELLA
(*waving*)

God bless you!   Buon viaggio!

FIORDILIGI

Ah see! Leaving the harbour   O Dei, come veloce

How the boat on the billows swiftly bears them.
Now it is seen no more. Safe be their journey
Both on land and on water!

Se ne va quella barca! Già sparisce.
Già non si vede più. Deh, faccia il cielo
Ch'abbia prospero corso.

DORABELLA

May the good Lord protect them
There on the field of slaughter!

Faccia che al campo giunga
Con fortunati auspici.

DON ALFONSO

And may peace and the victory at last restore them.

E a voi salvi gli amanti, a me gli amici.

FIORDILIGI, DORABELLA AND DON ALFONSO

No. 10 Terzettino

O wind gently blowing,
O'er ocean be playing,
O tide calmly flowing
Their barque be conveying
In peace to the shore;

Soave sia il vento,
Tranquilla sia l'onda,
Ed ogni elemento
Benigno risponda
Ai nostri desir.

O sun brightly shining
Shed happiness o'er them,
Be nature combining
Ere long to restore them
To greet us once more.

Soave sia il vento,
Tranquilla sia l'onda,
Ed ogni elemento
Benigno risponda
Ai nostri desir.

(The two women leave.)

Scene Seven. *Don Alfonso alone. / Secco Recitative*

DON ALFONSO

So far all's going successfully! By this time
The two devoted slaves of Mars and Venus
Are awaiting their 'orders'
For my own 'active service': now for the next scene
To bring them all together. Oh what faces,
Sighs and lamentations!
All the better for me,
It will make my task much easier:
Lonely hearts cannot fight such great temptation
For the odds are too heavy. I can assure you,
My poor misguided friends, I'm sorry for you.

Non son cattivo comico! Va bene ...
Al concertato loco i due campioni
Di Ciprigna e di Marte
Mi staranno attendendo: or senza indugio

Raggiungerli conviene. Quante smorfie,
Quante buffonerie!
Tanto meglio per me ...
Cadran più facilmente:
Questa razza di gente è la più presta
A cangiarsi d'umore. Oh, poverini!
Per femmina giocar cento zecchini?

Accompanied Recitative

He ploughs on water, sows where the sand confronts the wave,
And with a cobweb, holds the wind in custody,
Who all his hope reposes in women's loyalty.

Nel mare solca e nell'arena semina

E il vago vento spera in rete accogliere

Chi fonda sue speranze in cor di femina.

Scene Eight. *A pleasant room with two chairs, a little table, etc.. Three doors, two at the sides, and one at the back. Despina alone. / Secco Recitative*

DESPINA
(stirring her chocolate)

A hell of an existence
It is to be in service!
From morning till evening
You sweat, you labour and you worry,
And yet, for everything you do, no word of thanks.

Che vita maledetta
È il far la cameriera!
Dal mattino alla sera
Si fa, si suda, si lavora, e poi
Di tanto che si fa nulla è per noi.

Then the bell rings. I have	È mezz'ora che sbatto;
The chocolate ready and waiting. I have to make it	Il cioccolatte è fatto, ed a me tocca
Yet all that I'm allowed to do is smell it.	Restar ad odorarlo a secca bocca?
If the lady can drink it, why not the servant?	Non è forse la mia come la vostra,
They would soon give me notice —	O garbate signore,
An example of justice that takes the biscuit.	Che a voi dessi l'essenza e a me l'odore?
I wonder if they like it sweet	Perbacco, vo' assaggiarlo!
As this is!	Com'è buono!

(She tastes it and wipes her mouth.)

Here's someone.	Vien gente.
Oh heavens! Here come the ladies.	O ciel, son le padrone!

Scene Nine. *Despina, Fiordiligi and Dorabella. Fiordiligi and Dorabella enter in despair.*

DESPINA
(handing the cups of chocolate on a tray)

My ladies, here is your chocolate and biscuits.	Madame, ecco la vostra colazione.

(Dorabella throws everything on the floor.)

Heavens above! What's the matter?	Diamine! Cosa fate?

FIORDILIGI

Ah!   Ah!

DORABELLA

Ah!   Ah!

(Both women tear off their feminine adornments.)

DESPINA

What ever's happened?   Che cosa è nato?

FIORDILIGI

My griefs o'erwhelm me.	Ov'è un acciaro?
I am weary of life.	Un veleno dov'è?

DESPINA

What is it this time?   Padrone, dico!

Accompanied Recitative

DORABELLA

Beware of me lest in my wild affliction Some cruel hurt you suffer.	Ah, scostati! Paventa il triste effetto D'un disperato affetto!
Pull the blinds at the windows. Hateful the daylight, Hateful the air I am breathing, Hateful my being! Who can soothe my despair? Who will then console me?	Chiudi quelle finestre! Odio la luce, Odio l'aria che spiro, odio me stessa, Chi schernisce il mio duol, chi mi consola ...
Be gone for pity's sake, leave me here to die. Leave, I command you!	Deh, fuggi, per pietà, fuggi per pietà! Lasciatemi sola!

No. 11 Aria

Cease not, remorseless love,	[5]	Smanie implacabili
Thus to torment me,		Che m'agitate,
Furies from Phlegethon		Entro quest'anima
Still more oppress me;		Più non cessate
Pursue my anguish		Finchè l'angoscia
E'en unto death.		Mi fa morir!
You angry basilisks		Esempio misero
Consume my vitals.		D'amor funesto
Show the Eumenides,		Darò all'Eumenidi,
If I survive it,		Se viva resto,

71

How, in the toils of love,
I breathe my last.

Col suono orribile
De' miei sospir!

The two ladies seat themselves apart, distracted. / Secco Recitative

DESPINA

Signora Dorabella,
Signora Fiordiligi,
Tell me now, why this commotion?

Signora Dorabella,
Signora Fiordiligi,
Ditemi: che cosa è stato?

DORABELLA

Desolation and ruin!

Oh, terribil disgrazia!

DESPINA

That gives me no clear notion.

Sbrigatevi, in buonora!

FIORDILIGI

Our lovers have departed
Leaving us broken-hearted.

Da Napoli partiti
Sono gli amanti nostri.

DESPINA
(*laughing*)

Oh, is that all?
But they'll come back.

Non c'è altro?
Ritorneran.

DORABELLA

Who knows?

Chi sa!

DESPINA
(*as above*)

Why say 'who knows'?
Where have they gone to?

Come, chi sa?
Dove son iti?

DORABELLA

They've gone to fight a battle.

Al campo di battaglia.

DESPINA

All the better for them, then,
You will see them return loaded with
honours.

Tanto meglio per loro:
Li vedrete tornar carchi d'alloro.

FIORDILIGI

But what if they are killed?

Ma ponno anche perir.

DESPINA

If that should happen
All the better for you.

Allora, poi,
Tanto meglio per voi.

FIORDILIGI
(*rising angrily*)

What are you saying?

Sciocca! che dici?

DESPINA

I only speak the truth. If you lose these two,
There's plenty more to choose from.

La pura verità: due ne perdete,
Vi restan tutti gli altri.

FIORDILIGI

Ah, bereft of Guglielmo
I'd not be far behind him.

Ah, perdendo Guglielmo
Mi pare ch'io morrei!

DORABELLA

Ah, deprived of Ferrando
You'd quickly see me buried alive beside
him.

Ah, Ferrando perdendo
Mi par che viva a seppellirmi andrei!

72

Oh yes, of course, only just think: whoever
Heard of a woman dying of desolation?
Die of love for a man? If you should lose one,
Go at once and replace him.

Brave, 'vi par', ma non è ver: ancora
Non vi fu donna che d'amor sia morta.
Per un uomo morir! . . . Altri ve n'hanno
Che compensano il danno.

DORABELLA

A true and faithful woman
Can love but once if once she finds
  perfection:
Guglielmo or Ferrando.

E credi che potria
Altr'uomo amar chi s'ebbe per amante

Un Guglielmo, un Ferrando?

DESPINA

          Under correction
Every man has his equal;
You learn to love on one man,
And practice on the others: one's worth the
  other.
And all of them are worthless.
But surely you forget, though you are
  parted,
They live to plague you yet: don't be
  downhearted,
It's a little too soon to die
Of grief for the present;
Find something to amuse you!

         Han gli altri ancora
Tutto quello ch'han essi.
Un uomo adesso amate,
Un altro n'amerete: uno val l'altro,

Perchè nessun val nulla.
Ma non parliam di ciò: sono ancor vivi,

E vivi torneran; ma son lontani,

E, piuttosto che in vani
Pianti perdere il tempo,
Pensate a divertirvi.

FIORDILIGI
(*in a rage*)

      To amuse us?   Divertirci?

DESPINA

Why surely! Isn't it better
So to reflect your absent lovers?
They think a good deal about you,
  but do quite well without you.

Sicuro! E, quel ch'è meglio,
Far all'amor come assassine e come
Faranno al campo i vostri cari
  amanti.

DORABELLA

What a scandalous, wicked innuendo!
They will be true whatever others may be.

Non offender così quelle alme belle,
Di fedeltà, d'intatto amore esempi!

DESPINA

Come, come, give men their due!
A good lover's a man, and not a baby!

Via, via! Passaro i tempi
Da spacciar queste favole ai bambini!

No. 12 Aria

In gentlemen and in soldiers,
For constancy you look?

In uomini, in soldati
Sperare fedeltà?

(*laughing*)

I assure you you're totally mistook.

Non vi fate sentir, per carità!

For in reality,   [6]
Void of devotion,
Leaves ever fluttering,
Breezes in motion,
Waver no more than
The heart of a man.

Di pasta simile
Son tutti quanti:
Le fronde mobili,
L'aure incostanti
Han più degli uomini
Stabilità.

Tears of the crocodile,
Simpering faces,
Second-hand rhapsodies,
Crafty embraces,
From the beginning
Are part of their plan.

Mentite lagrime,
Fallaci sguardi,
Voci ingannevoli,
Vezzi bugiardi
Son le primarie
Lor qualità.

---

* The following two verses are often cut.

'What are the women for?	In noi non amano
Only for pleasure,'	Che 'l lor diletto;
Men are amused with them	Poi ci dispregiano,
Just at their leisure,	Neganci affetto,
Frown on or favour them	Nè val da' barbari
Quite as they please.	Chieder pietà.
Will you be trampled on,	Paghiam, o femmine,
Ladies, and bear it?	D'ugual moneta
This be your motto then,	Questa malefica
Up and declare it!	Razza indiscreta:
Flout them and jilt them	Amiam per comodo,
Whenever you can.	Per vanità!
La ra la, la ra la, la ra la, la.	La ra la, la ra la, la ra la, la.

(*They all leave.*)

Scene Ten. *Don Alfonso alone, then Despina. / Secco Recitative*

DON ALFONSO

What a silence! The very doors and windows	Che silenzio! che aspetto di tristezza
Share in the sad bereavement! Pretty darlings!	Spirano queste stanze! Poverette!
It's not entirely their fault.	Non han già tutto il torto:
I'll bring them consolation. Those simple youths	Bisogna consolarle. Infin che vanno
Will shortly be arriving,	I due creduli sposi,
The conspiracy aiding by masquerading.	Com'io loro commisi, a mascherarsi,
Let's think how to contrive it.	Pensiam cosa può farsi.
I must settle Despina: there's a danger	Temo un po' per Despina: quella furba
She might see through the masquerade — however	Potrebbe riconoscerli, potrebbe
I could do with some help from her. I'll risk it!	Rovesciarmi le macchine. Vedremo . . .
If I can only find her,	Se mai farà bisogno,
I know the way to treat her. A little money	Un regaletto a tempo: un zecchinetto
Will make the sourest girl as sweet as honey!	Per una cameriera è un gran scongiuro.
I'll make her my accomplice. Under pledge	Ma, per esser sicuro, si potria
Of secrecy, as my confidante I'll take her:	Metterla in parte a parte del segreto . . .
Yes, I think that's the best way.	Eccellente è il progetto . . .
Is she here? That's the question.	La sua camera è questa:

(*He knocks.*)

Despinetta!	Despinetta!

DESPINA

Who's calling?	Chi batte?

DON ALFONSO

Oh!	Oh!

DESPINA

Ah!	Ih!

DON ALFONSO

Pretty Despina,	Despina mia,
I need you rather badly.	Di te bisogno avrei.

DESPINA

But I've no need of you, dear.	Ed io niente di lei.

DON ALFONSO

I could do you some good.	Ti vo' fare del ben.

74

DESPINA

To a girl like me, dear,
Old gentlemen like you are worse than
  useless.

A una fanciulla
Un vecchio come lei non può far nulla.

DON ALFONSO

So you've no need of money.

Parla piano, ed osserva.

(*showing her a gold piece*)

DESPINA

Is that for me?

Me la dona?

DON ALFONSO

Yes, if you try to deserve it.

Si, se meco sei buona.

DESPINA

And how is that done?
You'll have to speak precisely.

E che vorrebbe?
È l'oro il mio giulebbe.

DON ALFONSO

I'm very glad to;
But you must be discreet.

Ed oro avrai;
Ma ci vuol fedeltà.

DESPINA

Nothing easier, go on.

Non c'è altro? Son qua.

DON ALFONSO

Here then: listen closely.
Persons I need not mention
Are bewailing their lovers.

Prendi, ed ascolta:
Sai che le tue padrone
Han perduto gli amanti.

DESPINA

I know.

Lo so.

DON ALFONSO

All they will do
Is wear themselves out in weeping and
  lamenting.

Tutti i lor pianti
Tutti i deliri loro anco tu sai.

DESPINA

For certain.

So tutto.

DON ALFONSO

All right, supposing
We find them consolation —
And what's a better kind than a flirtation?
So I have found two suitors
Who languish for the ladies
With the deepest affection.
They are also my friends and can be
  trusted.
I will add to my tip another guinea
If you join in the plan.

Orben, se mai,
Per consolarle un poco
E trar, come diciam, chiodo per chiodo,
Tu ritrovassi il modo
Da metter in lor grazia
Due soggetti di garbo
Che vorrieno provar . . . già mi capisci . . .

C'è una mancia per te di venti scudi,
Se li fai riuscir.

DESPINA*

I'm not unwilling
To accept this proposition.
And with those silly creatures — easy!
  But listen:
These friends of yours — they're handsome?
  And above all
Do they possess the money
To reinforce their ardour?

Non mi dispiace
Questa proposizione.
Ma con quelle buffone . . . Basta, udite:

Son giovani? Son belli? E, sopra tutto,

Hanno una buona borsa
I vostri concorrenti?

---

* These two verses are often cut in performance.

75

DON ALFONSO

They've all it takes to	Han tutto quello
Delight a girl. You will agree when you meet them.	Che piacer può alle donne di giudizio.
Shall we proceed?	Li vuoi veder?

DESPINA

Where are they now?	E dove son?

DON ALFONSO

Outside.	Son li.
Suppose I call them in.	Li posso far entrar?

DESPINA

Let them appear.	Direi di si.

(Don Alfonso brings in Ferrando and Guglielmo disguised.)

Scene Eleven. *Don Alfonso, Despina, Ferrando, Guglielmo; then Fiordiligi and Dorabella. / No. 13 Sextet*

DON ALFONSO

I've the honour to present you	Alla bella Despinetta
To the lady Despinetta,	Vi presento, amici miei;
And, if nothing can prevent you,	Non dipende che da lei
You yourselves can ask her aid.	Consolar il vostro cor.

FERRANDO AND GUGLIELMO
(with affected tenderness)

By this hand I kiss with pleasure,	Per la man che lieto io bacio,
Will you graciously allow me	Per quei rai di grazie pieni,
To behold the fair enchantress	Fa' che volga a me sereni
Who my heart has so enslaved?	I begli occhi il mio tesor.

DESPINA
(laughing to herself)

Lord preserve us, how peculiar!	Che sembianze! che vestiti!
Funny outfits, hairy features,	Che figure! che mustacchi!
Sure they must be foreign creatures,	Io non so se son valacchi,
I'd say Turkish at a guess.	O se turchi son costor.
Slovakish? Turkish?	Valacchi? Turchi?

DON ALFONSO
(aside to Despina)

What d'you think about their chances?	Che ti par di quell'aspetto?

DESPINA
(aside to Don Alfonso)

I'd be sick at their advances.	Per parlarvi schietto schietto,
Men so scarey and so hairy,	Hanno un muso fuor dell'uso,
Are an antidote to love.	Vero antidoto d'amor.

DON ALFONSO, FERRANDO AND GUGLIELMO
(aside)

Well, if she has no suspicion,	Ora la cosa è appien decisa:
There's no chance of recognition,	Se costei non $\left\{ \begin{array}{l} \text{li} \\ \text{ci} \end{array} \right.$ ravvisa
We have nothing now to fear.	Non c'è più nessun timor.

DESPINA
(aside, laughing)

Funny outfits and moustaches!	Che figure! che mustacchi!
I'd say something like Slovakish,	Io non so se son valacchi,
Or from Turkey at a guess.	O se turchi son costor.

FIORDILIGI AND DORABELLA
(*from within*)

Eh, Despina! Olà, Despina!   Ehi, Despina! Olà, Despina!

DESPINA

It's the ladies!   Le padrone!

DON ALFONSO
(*to Despina*)

Now is the moment!   Ecco l'istante!
No retreating: I'll join you later.   Fa' con arte: io qui m'ascondo.

(*He retires.*)

FIORDILIGI AND DORABELLA
(*entering*)

Wicked girl, this is an outrage!	Ragazzaccia tracotante,
You, with men, in conversation.	Che fai, lì, con simil gente?
Put an end to this intrusion,	Falli uscire immantinente,
We forbid their presence here.	O ti fo pentir con lor.

DESPINA, FERRANDO AND GUGLIELMO

Pardon, ladies, we implore you!	Ah, madame, perdonate!
Trembling here you see before you	Al bel piè languir mirate
Two poor things who would adore you,	Due meschin, di vostro merto
Love alone must bear the blame.	Spasimanti adorator.

FIORDILIGI AND DORABELLA

How insulting, how audacious!	Giusti Numi! cosa sento?
How insulting, how audacious!	Dell'enorme tradimento
Go! Begone, I blush for shame!	Chi fu mai l'indegno autor?

DESPINA, FERRANDO AND GUGLIELMO

But one moment, only hear us!   Deh, calmate quello sdegno ...

FIORDILIGI AND DORABELLA

No, begone and come not near us!	Ah, che più non ho ritegno!
Such discourteous provocation	Tutta piena ho l'alma in petto
Kindles fury in my heart.	Di dispetto e di furor!
Ah! My love, forgive this outrage,	Ah, perdon, mio bel diletto!
From afar defend my heart.	Innocente è questo cor.

FERRANDO AND GUGLIELMO
(*aside*)

Oh, enchanting! Their vexation	Qual diletto è a questo petto
Kindles rapture in my heart.	Quella rabbia e quel furor!

DESPINA AND DON ALFONSO
(*aside, Don Alfonso from the door*)

Most suspicious indignation!	Mi dà un poco di sospetto
Women always will act a part.	Quella rabbia e quel furor.

Secco Recitative

DON ALFONSO
(*as though entering*)

What an outcry! What infamy!	Che susurro! che strepito!
What a loud demonstration!	Che scompiglio è mai questo!
Are you crazy?	Siete pazze,
Calm yourselves girls, I beg you,	Care le mie ragazze?
The turmoil is attracting all	Volete sollevar il vicinato?
the neighbours.	
What's the matter? What's happened?	Cosa avete? che è nato?

DORABELLA
(furiously)

Dear friend, imagine.   Oh, ciel! Mirate:
Men! In this house of virtue.   Uomini in casa nostra!

DON ALFONSO
(without seeing the men)

What's wrong in that?   Che male c'è?

FIORDILIGI
(with excitement)

What's wrong? When tears engulf us? . . .   Che male? In questo giorno! . . .
To intrude uninvited?   Dopo il caso funesto! . . .

Accompanied Recitative

DON ALFONSO

Gracious! Goodness! Am I waking,   Stelle! Sogno o son desto? Amici
  or am I dreaming?   miei,
My old friends from the Balkans.   Miei dolcissimi amici!
You here? How so? Since when? How   Voi qui? Come? perchè? quando?
  long? What has brought you?   in qual modo?
Well, well, I am delighted!   Numi! Quanto ne godo!

(aside to them / Secco Recitative)

Do play up to me.   Secondatemi.

FERRANDO

It can't be Don Alfonso!   Amico Don Alfonso!

GUGLIELMO

Our dear old tutor!   Amico caro!

(They embrace him with enthusiasm.)

DON ALFONSO

Most unexpected meeting!   Oh, che bella improvvisata!

DESPINA
(to Don Alfonso)

You've met these men before?   Li conoscete, voi?

DON ALFONSO

Of course I've met them! They're   Se li conosco! Questi
The cleverest of my pupils,   Sono i più dolci amici
And best of good companions;   Ch'io m'abbia in questo mondo,
As you will find them also.   E vostri ancor saranno.

FIORDILIGI

But why are they in our house?   E in casa mia che fanno?

GUGLIELMO

                  It was a liberty   Ai vostri piedi
We know: but if you ask what force   Due rei, due delinquenti, ecco,
  hither brought us . . .   madame!

Accompanied Recitative

'Twas Love!   Amor.

FIORDILIGI

Heavens, be silent!   . Numi! Che sento!

FERRANDO

                  Yes, Love, or rather   Amor, il Nume
You yourselves were the force that hither   Si possente, per voi qui ci conduce.
  brought us.

78

(The ladies retreat, pursued by the men.)

GUGLIELMO

We had scarce apprehended The incandescent sunlight of your glances . . .	. . . Vista appena la luce Di vostre fulgidissime pupille . . .

FERRANDO

. . . Than like moths to a lantern . . .	. . . Che alle vive faville . . .

GUGLIELMO

. . . Or like butterflies mad with love, and dying . . .	. . . Farfallette amorose e agonizzanti . . .

FERRANDO

. . . We come fluttering before you . . .	. . . Vi voliamo davanti . . .

GUGLIELMO

. . . And behind and around you . . .	. . . Ed ai lati, ed a retro . . .

FERRANDO AND GUGLIELMO

. . . To crave your kind compassion or else to perish!	. . . Per implorar pietade in flebil metro!

FIORDILIGI

How could they dare!	Stelle! Che ardir!

DORABELLA

I know not what to answer.	Sorella, che facciamo?

(Despina leaves, frightened.)

FIORDILIGI

Bold intruders, quickly Begone from this house of virtue! Do not profane us With the base words of your detested homage Or our hearts, or our hearing, or our affection. In vain for you or any other, to threaten To assail our resolve. Our troth untainted We have solemnly plighted to absent lovers: We to them will remain faithful for ever, In the face of all danger steadfast together.	Temerari! sortite Fuori di questo loco! E non profani L'alito infausto degl'infami detti Nostro cor, nostro orecchio e nostri affetti! Invan per voi, per gli altri invan si cerca Le nostre alme sedur: l'intatta fede Che per noi già si diede ai cari amanti Saprem loro serbar infino a morte, A dispetto del mondo e della sorte.

No. 14 Aria

Like a fortress in ocean founded, Though the billows may surge around it, So my heart relies undaunted On its virtue and on its love.	Come scoglio immoto resta Contro i venti e la tempesta, Così ognor quest'alma è forte Nella fede e nell'amor.
There's a strength in vows, once plighted, (Happy lovers who have found it!) Fate and silent stars united, Love's devotion cannot move!	Con noi nacque quella face Che ci piace e ci consola; E potrà la morte sola Far che cangi affetto il cor.
Have respect, you rash intruders, And refrain from self-delusion, May our constancy unbounded Warning and example prove!	Rispettate, anime ingrate, Questo esempio di costanza; E una barbara speranza Non vi renda audaci ancor.

The ladies prepare to leave. Ferrando calls Fiordiligi back, Guglielmo calls Dorabella. / Secco Recitative

FERRANDO

Stay, I implore you!	Ah, non partite!

GUGLIELMO
(to Dorabella)

Remain with us, I beg you.	Ah, barbara, restate!

(aside, to Don Alfonso)

What do you think?	Che vi pare?

DON ALFONSO
(aside to Guglielmo)

They're not gone yet.	Aspettate!

(to the ladies)

They've chosen the wrong moment,	Per carità, ragazze,
But from kindness to me, do not refuse them.	Non mi fate più far trista figura!

DORABELLA
(angrily)

And what makes you excuse them?	E che pretendereste?

DON ALFONSO

Oh! Nothing; if you knew them	Eh, nulla ... Ma mi pare ...
You would greet with more kindness	Che un pochin di dolcezza ...
Two men who are so talented ...	Alfin, son galantuomini
I've known them for a long time.	E sono amici miei.

FIORDILIGI

But why, what good can we do them?	Come! E udire dovrei ...

GUGLIELMO

It's your acquaintance	Le nostre pene
We have come here to make.	E sentirne pietà!
It was only the chance of humbly pleading	La celeste beltà degli occhi vostri
The cause of hearts fast bleeding!	La piaga apri nei nostri
It's you alone can save them	Cui rimediar può solo
Or heal the wounds you gave them:	Il balsamo d'amore.
From lip of beauty the love that craved a trial	Un solo istante il core aprite, o belle,
Never met with denial: you see before you	A sue dolci facelle, o a voi davanti
The men of all men who live but to adore you!	Spirar vedrete i più fedeli amanti.

*No. 15 Aria**

O vision so charming,	[7]	Non siate ritrosi,
Your anger disarming,		Occhietti vezzosi:
With sympathy warming		Due lampi amorosi
Deign on us to shine!		Vibrate un po' qua.

Whate'er you may bestow on us	Felici rendeteci,
We doubly will render,	Amate con noi,
With passion as impetuous,	E noi felicissime
And blandishment as tender.	Faremo anche voi.

No longer reject us!	Guardate, toccate,
Come near and inspect us!	Il tutto osservate.
Please state your objection	Siam due cari matti,
To form or complexion,	Siam forti e ben fatti,
Suggest an improvement	E, come ognun vede,
In figure or poses –	Sia merito o caso,
We're proud of our ankles,	Abbiamo bel piede,
Our eyebrows, our noses,	Bell'occhio, bel naso;
These noble moustaches,	E questi mustacchi
The latest in fashion,	Chiamare si possono
Expressive of passion	Trionfi degli uomini,
Seductively twine!	Pennacchi d'amor.

(The ladies leave in anger.)

---

* Before the first performance in 1789, Mozart substituted this aria for the original aria written for Benucci *'Rivolgete a lui lo sguardo'* which may be found on page 124.

Scene Twelve. *Ferrando, Guglielmo and Don Alfonso. The two lovers laugh heartily, mocking Don Alfonso.* / *No. 16 Terzetto*

DON ALFONSO

You seem delighted!   E voi ridete?

FERRANDO AND GUGLIELMO

Yes, we're delighted.   Certo, ridiamo.

DON ALFONSO

Downright excited!   Ma cosa avete?

FERRANDO AND GUGLIELMO

Downright excited.   Già lo sappiamo.

DON ALFONSO

You laugh too early.   Ridete piano!

FERRANDO AND GUGLIELMO

Don't be so surly.   Parlate invano!

DON ALFONSO

Laughter so clamorous,   Se vi sentissero,
From men so amorous,   Se vi scoprissero,
Will call attention   Si guasterebbe
If they should hear!   Tutto l'affar.

(aside)

You're too uproarious,   Mi fa da ridere
Don't be vainglorious,   Questo lor ridere,
Premature laughter   Ma so che in piangere
Oft ends in a tear.   Dee terminar.

FERRANDO AND GUGLIELMO
(laughing aside, trying not to laugh)

They're inconsolable!   Ah, che dal ridere
Mirth uncontrollable   L'alma dividere,
Must have its way,   Ah, che le viscere
For there's nobody near.   Sento scoppiar!

Secco Recitative

DON ALFONSO

When you've quite finished laughing   Si può sapere un poco
Will you say what the joke is?   La cagion di quel riso?

GUGLIELMO

Oh, what a question!   Oh, cospettaccio!
You will see, and perhaps you will believe   Non vi pare che abbiam giusta ragione,
us
When we've lightened your purse.   Il mio caro padrone?

FERRANDO
(playfully)

Tell us, how much you'll give us   Quanto pagar volete,
To settle up the wager!   E a monte è la scommessa?

GUGLIELMO
(playfully)

We'll let you off with half!   Pagate la metà!

FERRANDO
(as before)

Or out of friendship   Pagate solo
Be content with a quarter.   Ventiquattro zecchini!

DON ALFONSO

Ah, my poor young innocents,	Poveri innocentini!
Pray have your laugh! I still	Venite qua: vi voglio
Intend to win my wager.	Porre il ditino in bocca!

GUGLIELMO

The bet remains then?	E avete ancora
Your fate you still defy?	Coraggio di fiatar?

DON ALFONSO

We'd better talk	Avanti sera
Of that bye and bye.	Ci parlerem.

FERRANDO

We shall be ready!	Quando volete!

DON ALFONSO

Again then,	Intanto,
I hold you at my command	Silenzio e ubbidienza
Till tomorrow morning.	Fino a doman mattina.

GUGLIELMO

Are we not soldiers? We need no second warning.	Siamo soldati, e amiam la disciplina.

DON ALFONSO

Exactly. And for my next trick	Orbene, andate un poco
The seducers confront them in the garden;	Ad attendermi entrambi in giardinetto:
The strategy I'll tell you when we get there.	Colà vi manderò gli ordini miei.

GUGLIELMO

And what about our dinner?	Ed oggi non si mangia?

FERRANDO

Does it matter?	Cosa serve?
When the battle is over	A battaglia finita
Then the feast we'll enjoy will last for ever.	Fia la cena per noi più saporita.

No. 17 Aria

From eyes so alluring	[8]	Un'aura amorosa
Our hope reassuring		Del nostro tesoro
A mystic refreshment		Un dolce ristoro
Our hearts will beguile;		Al cor porgerà;
For hearts that are nourished,		Al cor che, nudrito
On longing and passion,		Da speme, da amore,
A glance is ambrosia,		Di un'esca migliore
And nectar a smile.		Bisogno non ha.

(Ferrando and Guglielmo leave.)

Scene Thirteen. *Don Alfonso alone, then Despina. / Secco Recitative*

DON ALFONSO

This is indeed a miracle! For, since	Oh, la saria da ridere: sì poche
The world began, so few women yet were constant.	Son le donne costanti, in questo mondo,
They tell me here are two! I don't believe it!	E qui ve ne son due! Non sarà nulla ...

(Despina enters.)

Ah, you're there Despinetta, I've something to ask you.	Vieni, vieni, fanciulla, e dimmi un poco
Can you tell me, what's become of your young ladies.	Dove sono e che fan le tue padrone.

DESPINA

The silly little creatures	Le povere buffone
Are wandering in the garden	Stanno nel giardinetto

And repine with the breezes (and the mosquitoes)	A lagnarsi coll'aria e colle mosche
For their lovers' departure.	D'aver perso gli amanti.

DON ALFONSO

What's your opinion?	E come credi
Will we fail in our plot? Will they be faithful?	Che l'affar finirà? Vogliam sperare
Are they women or not?	Che faranno giudizio?

DESPINA*

Totally female.	Io lo farei;
And they are bound to show it! Instead of weeping	E dove piangon esse io riderei,
There'll be laughter! Such folly	Disperarsi, strozzarsi
Thus to starve midst of plenty	Perchè parte un amante?
When, if they did but know it,	Guardate che pazzia!
Any lover may be replaced with twenty!	Se ne pigliano due, s'uno va via.

DON ALFONSO

Brava! Sound sense and reason!	Brava, questa è prudenza!
	(aside)
A compliment in season!	Bisogna impuntigliarla.

DESPINA

It is a law of nature,	È legge di natura,
A fact surpassing reason, for what is love?	E non prudenza sola. Amor cos'è?
It's joy, luxury, comfort,	Piacer, comodo, gusto,
Passion, imagination,	Gioia, divertimento,
Expectation, and romance; but when it switches	Passatempo, allegria: non è più amore,
To pain instead of pleasure,	Se incomodo diventa,
Then it's no longer Love, it's merely folly!	Si invece di piacer nuoce e tormenta.

DON ALFONSO

And these two charmers on trial?	Ma intanto queste pazze ...

DESPINA

Not a hope!	Quelle pazze
The verdict will be 'Guilty'. We will bring evidence	Faranno a modo nostro. È buon che sappiano
To show the Plaintiffs are their suitors.	D'esser amate da color.

DON ALFONSO

They know it!	Lo sanno.

DESPINA

Then must the Suit be pleaded –	Dunque riameranno.
Each for himself as 'Counsel',	'Diglielo', si suol dire,
With us for their 'Solicitors'.	'E lascia fare al diavolo.'

DON ALFONSO

Then tell me,	Ma come
Have you a plan that's feasible –	Far vuoi perchè ritornino,
Now that my friends have left them – to bring them back again	Or che partiti sono, e che li sentano
To that problem in petticoats	E tentare si lascino,
Whom we may call 'Defendants'?	Queste tue bestioline?

DESPINA

To bring them back will	A me lasciate
Be easy; you may trust to me to manage it.	La briga di condur tutta la macchina.
Since you have taken me for ally and partner,	Quando Despina macchina una cosa

---

* The rest of this scene is often considerably cut in performance.

I'll see you don't repent it! If men by dozens	Non può mancar d'effetto: ho già menati
A match for them have found me,	Mill'uomini pel naso,
Shall two mere females baffle me? Have they money?	Saprò menar due femmine. Son ricchi
These two bewhiskered suitors?	I due monsù mustacchi?

DON ALFONSO

They are made of it.	Son ricchissimi.

DESPINA

And where are they?	Dove son?

DON ALFONSO

Round the corner,	Sulla strada
And waiting my signal.	Attendendo mi stanno.

DESPINA

All right, go and fetch them;	Ite, e sul fatto
Bring them round to the house	Per la picciola porta
Through the door behind the shrubbery. I'll find you	A me riconduceteli; v'aspetto
In the room near the garden.	Nella camera mia.
If only they are willing	Purchè tutto facciate
To carry out my plan, before tomorrow	Quel ch'io v'ordinerò, pria di domani
Your funny friends will celebrate a victory;	I vostri amici canteran vittoria;
The men shall win the ladies and I the glory.	Ed essi avranno il gusto, ed io la gloria.

(They leave.)

Scene Fourteen. *A pretty little garden with a grass bank at each side. Fiordiligi and Dorabella. / No. 18 Finale*

FIORDILIGI AND DORABELLA

Why has fate my life enshrouded	Ah, che tutta in un momento
In a mystery of sorrow?	Si cangiò la sorte mia . . .
Why are happy days o'erclouded	Ah, che un mar pien di tormento
By a gloomy haze of care?	È la vita omai per me!
Ah! While he was there to cheer me	Finchè meco il caro bene
Brighter yet rose every morrow,	Mi lasciar le ingrate stelle,
Never shade of grief came near me,	Non sapea cos'eran pene,
All was well, for he was there.	Non sapea languir cos'è.
Why has fate my life enshrouded	Ah, che tutta in un momento
In a mystery of sorrow?	Si cangiò la sorte mia . . .
Why are happy days o'erclouded	Ah, che un mar pien di tormento
By a gloomy haze of care?	È la vita omai per me!

Scene Fifteen. *Fiordiligi, Dorabella, Guglielmo and Don Alfonso; then Despina.*

FERRANDO AND GUGLIELMO
(off-stage)

To die is all I long for	Si mora, sì, si mora
Rather than this distraction.	Onde appagar le ingrate!

DON ALFONSO
(off-stage)

Your patience must be stronger:	C'è una speranza ancora:
Forbear the fatal action!	Non fate, o Dei, non fate!

FIORDILIGI AND DORABELLA

Heavens, they do sound desperate!	Stelle, che grida orribili!

FERRANDO AND GUGLIELMO

Let go of me!	Lasciatemi!

DON ALFONSO

Do be patient!	Aspettate!

84

(Enter Ferrando and Guglielmo, each carrying a small bottle, followed by Don Alfonso.)

FERRANDO AND GUGLIELMO

This arsenic contains the power	L'arsenico mi liberi
To end my cruel pains!	Di tanta crudeltà!

(They drink, and throw away the bottles. Turning round they see the two ladies.)

FIORDILIGI AND DORABELLA

Can they be taking poison?	Stelle! Un velen fu quello?

DON ALFONSO

Alas! There's no denying	Veleno buono e bello
Their last half hour is flying,	Che ad essi in pochi istanti
No hope of life remains!	La vita toglierà.

FIORDILIGI AND DORABELLA

Oh, what a tragic spectacle!	Il tragico spettacolo
My heart is frozen quite.	Gelare il cor mi fa.

FERRANDO AND GUGLIELMO

You are the ones responsible.	Barbare, avvicinatevi:
Yet sweet the bitter potion	D'un disperato affetto
If you our life's devotion	Mirate il tristo effetto
With one last look requite.	E abbiate almen pietà.

FIORDILIGI AND DORABELLA

Oh, what a tragic spectacle!	Il tragico spettacolo
My heart is frozen quite.	Gelare il cor mi fa.

FIORDILIGI, DORABELLA, FERRANDO, GUGLIELMO AND DON ALFONSO

Oh, that the night would cover me,	Ah, che del sole il raggio
Veiling the awful horror.	Fosco per me diventa.
Coldness and anguish come over me,	Tremo le fibre, e l'anima
Feeling and sight are failing,	Par che mancar si senta,
My heart with terror is quailing,	Ne può la lingua o il labbro
To speak I know not how.	Accenti articolar!

(Ferrando and Guglielmo fall onto the grass banks.)

DON ALFONSO

Can you behold them dying?	Giacchè a morir vicini
Never a word replying?	Sono quei meschinelli,
If only for a moment	Pietade almeno a quelli
Some little pity show.	Cercate di mostrar.

FIORDILIGI AND DORABELLA

Help us, help us, will no-one hear us?	Gente, accorrete, gente!
Alas! There's no-one near us!	Nessuno, oddio, ci sente!
Despina!	Despina!

DESPINA
(off-stage)

Just a minute.	Chi mi chiama?

FIORDILIGI AND DORABELLA

Despina!	Despina!

DESPINA
(entering)

What's the matter?	Cosa vedo!
Ah, what a sight appalling!	Morti i meschini io credo,
Is this what Fate decreed?	O prossimi a spirar.

DON ALFONSO

Oh, 'twas a deed unhallowed!	Ah, che purtroppo è vero!
The deadly poison swallowed	Furenti, disperati,

And throes of anguish followed!
Oh, this was love indeed!

Si sono avvelenati,
Oh, amore singolar!

DESPINA

Well, in this sad extremity,
It's folly most amazing
To stand here idly gazing.

Abbandonar i miseri
Saria per voi vergogna:
Soccorrerli bisogna.

FIORDILIGI, DORABELLA AND DON ALFONSO

Yes, but what can we do?

Cosa possiam mai far?

DESPINA

Some life is still remaining,
Tenderly support them,
Try to restore the feeling.

Di vita ancor dan segno:
Colle pietose mani
Fate un po' lor sostegno.

(to Don Alfonso)

We'll leave you here to watch them
While we for aid or remedy
In frantic haste will run.

E voi con me correte:
Un medico, un antidoto
Voliamo a ricercar.

(Despina and Don Alfonso leave.)

FIORDILIGI AND DORABELLA

Never was fate so spiteful!

Dei, che cimento è questo!

An action half so frightful
Was never seen or heard!

Evento più funesto
Non si potea trovar!

FERRANDO AND GUGLIELMO
(aside)

This farce is too delightful!
I would not miss a word!

Più belle commediola
Non si potea trovar!

(sighing aloud)

Ah!

Ah!

FIORDILIGI AND DORABELLA
(standing at a distance from the men)

The wretched things are sighing!   Sospiram gli infelici!

FIORDILIGI

What should we do?

Che facciamo?

DORABELLA

Are they dying?   Tu che dici?

FIORDILIGI

I suppose in such conditions
Some support we ought to give.

In momenti si dolenti,
Chi potriali abbandonar?

DORABELLA
(approaching a little)

They've a certain strange attraction.   Che figure interessanti!

FIORDILIGI
(approaching a little)

Surely there's a case for action!   Possiam farci un poco avanti.

DORABELLA

Ah, how cold, how cold his skin is!   Ha freddissima la testa.

FIORDILIGI

Nothing like as cold as mine is!   Fredda fredda e ancora questa.

DORABELLA

Does his heart beat?   Ed il polso?

FIORDILIGI

Not even slightly.	Io non gliel sento.

DORABELLA

This one's beating very lightly.	Questo batte lento lento.

FIORDILIGI AND DORABELLA

Ah! If help is long arriving	Ah, se tarda ancor l'aita,
There's no hope of their surviving.	Speme più non v'è di vita.

FERRANDO AND GUGLIELMO
(*aside*)

See how kindly and compassionate	Più domestiche e trattabili
They are gradually becoming.	Sono entrambe diventate.
We shall see them soon relenting,	Sta' a veder che lor pietate
Pity is akin to love.	Va in amore a terminar.

FIORDILIGI AND DORABELLA

This disaster most appalling	Poverini! La lor morte
Must the heart to pity move.	Mi farebbe lagrimar.

Scene Sixteen. *Fiordiligi, Dorabella, Ferrando, Guglielmo, Despina disguised as a doctor, and Don Alfonso.*

DON ALFONSO

Now, ladies, calm yourselves.	Eccovi il medico,
Here's the physician!	Signore belle.

FERRANDO AND GUGLIELMO
(*aside*)

A clever masquerade,	Despina in maschera!
It is Despina.	Che trista pelle!

DESPINA

Salvete, amabiles	*Salvete, amabiles*
Bones puellae!	*Bones puelles!**

FIORDILIGI AND DORABELLA

His speech is quite beyond	Parla un linguaggio
Our comprehension!	Che non sappiamo.

DESPINA

You've but to order me	Come comandano,
What I shall speak in:	Dunque, parliamo:
From Dutch to Syrian,	So il greco e l'arabo,
Welsh or Illyrian,	So il turco e il vandalo;
Celtic or Arabic,	Lo svevo e il tartaro
Greek or Hindu.	So ancor parlar.

DON ALFONSO

So many languages	Tanti linguaggi
Are quite unneeded.	Per sè conservi.
Matters more serious	Quei miserabili
Wait your attention.	Per ora osservi:
They've taken arsenic,	Preso hanno il tossico,
What shall we do?	Che si può far?

FIORDILIGI AND DORABELLA

Tell us, good doctor,	Signor dottore,
What shall we do?	Che si può far?

DESPINA
(*She feels the pulse and the brow of one and then the other.*)

Can you explain to me,	Saper bisognami

---

* The libretto has 'Bonae puellae' but the score has 'Bones puelles' — Mozart's joke?

For information,	Pria la cagione,
Tell me how big a dose	E quinci l'indole
That they have taken!	Della pozione:
A teaspoon, a tablespoon?	Se calda o frigida,
A capsule, a bottle?	Se poca o molta,
Was it diluted	Se in una volta
Or was it pure?	Ovvero in più.

FIORDILIGI, DORABELLA AND DON ALFONSO

They've taken arsenic	Preso han l'arsenico,
Straight from the bottle.	Signor dottore:
Took it internally,	Qui dentro il bevvero,
Caused them to mottle	La causa è amore,
And in a moment	Ed in un sorso
Fall on the floor.	Se 'l mandar giù.

DESPINA

Don't get excited	Non vi affannate,
Or overheated;	Non vi turbate:
Just pay attention	Ecco una prova
To what I do.	Di mia virtù.

FIORDILIGI, DORABELLA AND DON ALFONSO

He's got a magnet,	Egli ha di un ferro
How will he use it?	La man fornita.

DESPINA
(She touches each mock invalid on the head with a magnet and pulls it along their bodies.)

I am a pupil of	Questo è quel pazzo
Doctor Mesmer,	Di calamita,
And he invented it.	Pietra Mesmerica,
In its simplicity,	Ch'ebbe l'origine
Passing in mystery	Nell'Alemagna,
All facts of history,	Che poi si celebre
Is all his own!	Là in Francia fu.

FIORDILIGI, DORABELLA AND DON ALFONSO

See, they are quivering,	Come si muovono,
Shivering, chattering,	Torcono, scuotono!
Now on the footpath	In terra il cranio
Their skulls are battering.	Presto percuotono.

DESPINA

You must support them,	Ah, lor la fronte
Firmly and true.	Tenete su.

FIORDILIGI AND DORABELLA

See, we are ready!	Eccoci pronte.

(They put their hands on the men's brows.)

DESPINA

Support them strongly!	Tenete forte.
Tremendous! The cure has worked!	Coraggio! Or liberi
Death is defeated!	Siete da morte.

FIORDILIGI, DORABELLA AND DON ALFONSO

See, they revive again,	Attorno guardano,
Movement they make again!	Forze reprendono ...
Such a physician's worth	Ah, questo medico
All of Peru!	Vale un Perù!

FERRANDO AND GUGLIELMO
(getting to their feet)

Where is this? What heavenly region?	Dove son? che loco è questo?
Who is he, serene and mighty?	Chi è colui? color chi sono?
Do I wake in realms Elysian?	Son di Giove innanzi al trono?

(Ferrando to Fiordiligi and Guglielmo to Dorabella)

Are you Pallas or Aphrodite?	Sei tu Palla o Citerea?
No, it's you my fair enslaver.	No ... tu sei l'alma mia Dea:
Yours the charm my limbs enchaining;	Ti ravviso al dolce viso
If my pains can win your favour,	E alla man ch'or ben conosco
Grant me torment more intense!	E che sola è il mio tesor.

(They embrace the ladies tenderly and kiss their hands.)

DESPINA AND DON ALFONSO
(to the ladies)

Slight derangement still remaining;	Son effetti ancor del tosco:
They intend you no offence.	Non abbiate alcun timor.

FIORDILIGI AND DORABELLA

That may be, but such extravagance	Sarà ver, ma tante smorfie
Savours more of base pretence.	Fanno torto al nostro onor.

FERRANDO AND GUGLIELMO
(aside, while the others repeat their verses)

Now is laughter uncontrollable.	Della voglia ch'ho di ridere
What delightful innocence!	Il polmon mi scoppia or or.

(Ferrando to Fiordiligi and Guglielmo to Dorabella)

Goddess, must you scorn undo me?	Per pietà, bell'idol mio ...

FIORDILIGI AND DORABELLA

Oh, why will he thus pursue me?	Più resister non poss'io.

FERRANDO AND GUGLIELMO
(to the ladies)

Will you not with smiles renew me?	Volgi a me le luci liete!

(aside)

Now is laughter uncontrollable.	Dalla voglia ch'ho di ridere
What delightful innocence!	Il polmon mi scoppia or or.

(to the ladies)

Let me kiss you e'er I perish,	Dammi un bacio, o mio tesoro;
Just one kiss for me to cherish.	Un sol bacio, o qui mi moro!

FIORDILIGI AND DORABELLA

Heavens! He'd kiss me?	Stelle! Un bacio?

DESPINA AND DON ALFONSO
(to the ladies)

Wretched creatures!	Secondate
Just one act of pure good nature!	Per effetto di bontate.

FIORDILIGI AND DORABELLA

Such a thing a modest woman	Ah, che troppo si richiede
Would consent to do for no-one.	Da una fida, onesta amante.
It's an insult to my sadness,	Oltraggiata è la mia fede,
It's an insult to my love!	Oltraggiato è questo cor!

DESPINA AND DON ALFONSO
(aside)

Here's a tableau most amusing,	Un quadretto più giocondo
Men desiring and girls refusing,	Non si vide in tutto il mondo.
Nothing could be more { confusing / ridiculous	Quel che più mi fa da ridere
Than this anger and all this fuss.	È quell'ira e quel furor.

FERRANDO AND GUGLIELMO
(aside)

Here's a tableau most amusing,	Un quadretto più giocondo
Men desiring and girls refusing,	Non s'è visto, in questo mondo.
Nothing could be more { confusing / ridiculous	Ma non so se finta o vera
Than this anger and all this fuss.	Sia quell'ira e quel furor.

89

Say no more, the Devil take you!
May the poison madder make you!
Or if love be worse than madness
Not a pang will we allay.

Disperati, attossicati,
Ite al diavol quanti siete!
Tardi inver vi pentirete,
Se più cresce il mio furor!

(The sisters repeat this verse while the other four sing as follows.)

DESPINA AND DON ALFONSO
(aside)

Here's a tableau most amusing,
Men desiring, girls refusing,
Nothing could be more ridiculous
Than this anger and all this fuss.
It is all dissimulation:
Women's ways too well I know.

Un quadretto più giocondo
Non si vide in tutto il mondo.
Quel che più mi fa da ridere
È quell'ira e quel furor,
Ch'io ben so che tanto fuoco
Cangerassi in quel d'amor.

FERRANDO AND GUGLIELMO
(aside)

Here's a tableau most amusing,
Men desiring, girls refusing,
Nothing could be more confusing
Than this anger and all this fuss.
Great would be my indignation
Were they not to answer 'No'.

Un quadretto più giocondo
Non s'è visto, in questo mondo.
Ma non so se finta o vera
Sia quell'ira e quel furor.
Nè vorrei che tanto fuoco
Terminasse in quel d'amor.

End of the First Act.

Act Two

Scene One. *A room. Fiordiligi, Dorabella and Despina. / Secco Recitative*

DESPINA

Well, I declare, you are	Andate là, che siete
A funny pair of young ladies!	Due bizzarre ragazze!

FIORDILIGI

Oh, do be quiet!	Oh, cospettaccio!
What have we got to laugh at?	Cosa pretenderesti?

DESPINA

Not at me, Miss!	Per me nulla.

FIORDILIGI

Well, at what then?	Per chi, dunque?

DESPINA

Yourselves.	Per voi.

DORABELLA

Ourselves?	Per noi?

DESPINA

Yourselves!	Per voi:
Are you women, or not?	Siete voi donne, o no?

FIORDILIGI

What a question!	E per questo?

DESPINA

'What a question!'	'E per questo!'
You must behave like women.	Dovete far da donne.

DORABELLA

How's that?	Cioè?

DESPINA

By treating love as a diversion:	Trattar l'amore *en bagatelle:*
If the moment offers	Le occasioni belle
Don't neglect a good chance. Sometimes be fickle,	Non negliger giammai; cangiar a tempo,
At other times be constant.	A tempo esser costanti;
Be formal or coquettish,	*Coquettizzar* con grazia;
But avoid the disgrace that comes when maidens	Prevenir la disgrazia, si comune
Believe that men have scruples;	A chi si fida in uomo;
Enjoy the figs, but don't discard the apples.	Magiar il fico e non gittare il pomo.

FIORDILIGI
(aside)

You horrid girl!	Che diavole!

(to Despina)

That's very fine	Tai cose
For you, if you dare to.	Falle tu, se n'hai voglia.

DESPINA

I often dare to!	Io già le faccio.
It's no different for you:	Ma vorrei che anche voi,
Remind them that a woman	Per gloria del bel sesso,
Is every bit as human. For example,	Faceste un po' lo stesso. Per esempio:

By talk to action suiting,
They were soldiers who left you, so show your sympathy
With military matters, by recruiting!

I vostri ganimedi
Son andati alla guerra? Infin che tornano,

Fate alla militare: reclutate.

DORABELLA

They march with Heaven's protection.

Il cielo ce ne guardi!

DESPINA

But meanwhile we're on earth and not in heaven!
You've one plain fact before you; there are others
Who adore you. They long for you —
Do let them have their way!
Gentlemen, full of passion! Don Alfonso
Gave them good testimonials; you've seen that at
Your door their death might be laid, if you should scorn them.
With the charms that adorn them,
Why can you not behave as is the fashion?
It's the suit women crave, more than the suitor.

Eh, che noi siamo in terra, e non in cielo!
Fidatevi al mio zelo giacchè questi

Forastieri v'adorano,
Lasciatevi adorar. Son ricchi, belli,
Nobili, generosi, come fede
Fece a voi Don Alfonso; avean coraggio

Di morire per voi: questi son merti

Che sprezzar non si denno
Da giovani qual voi belle e galanti,
Che pon star senza amor, non senza amanti.

(aside)

Truly they like their tutor!

Par che ci trovin gusto.

FIORDILIGI

Do think what you are saying,
How could you be so thoughtless?
Do you think we'll attend you?
Why should our house provide idle gossip?
We'd risk our lovers' anger,
And their faith in our vows rashly endanger?

Perbacco, ci faresti
Far delle belle cose!
Credi tu che vogliamo
Favola diventar degli oziosi?
Ai nostri cari sposi
Credi tu che vogliam dar tal tormento?

DESPINA

Do you think they would cherish
Such unworthy suspicion?

E chi dice che abbiate
A far loro alcun torto?

DORABELLA

Reputation with ladies of position
Unprotected as we are,
By a slander may perish.

Non ti pare che sia torto bastante,
Se noto si facesse
Che trattiamo costor?

DESPINA

As far as that goes,
The risk is not too serious.
Should there be any chatter,
The men were after me.

Anche per questo
C'è un mezzo sicurissimo:
Io voglio sparger fama
Che vengono da me.

DORABELLA

Who would believe that?

Chi vuoi che il creda?

DESPINA

Oh, thank you! Is a maid not
Good enough to have a beau,
Or two if she can get them? Trust me to handle it.

Oh, bella! Non ha forse
Merto una cameriera
D'aver due cicisbei? Di me fidatevi.

FIORDILIGI

No, no, to be so crafty
Would endanger our image:
The men we might have pitied,
But they tried to embrace us.

No, no: son troppo audaci,
Questi tuoi forastieri.
Non ebber la baldanza
Fin di chieder dei baci?

92

DESPINA
(*aside*)

Very shocking!   Che disgrazia!

(*to the ladies*)

It's nonsense what you're thinking;	Io posso assicurarvi
You could see that their action	Che le cose che han fatto
Was brought on by the stuff they had been drinking —	Furo effetti del tossico che han preso:
With convulsion, delirium,	Convulsioni, deliri,
Delusion, severe distraction.	Follie, vaneggiamenti.
Now you'll see how circumstances alter.	Ma or vedrete come son discreti,
Though admiring, they're modest and retiring;	Manierosi, modesti e mansueti.
Do let them call today.	Lasciateli venir.

DORABELLA

And then?   E poi?

DESPINA

And then!   E poi . . .

Join them in conversation!   Caspita! Fate voi!

(*aside*)

Down go the first defences.   L'ho detto che cadrebbero.

FIORDILIGI

What could we find to say?   Cosa dobbiamo far?

DESPINA

Don't try to plan it!   Quel che volete:

You have less imagination than blocks of granite!   Siete d'ossa e di carne, o cosa siete?

No. 19 Aria

At fifteen a girl already	[9]	Una donna a quindici anni
Must be truly wise and worldly.		Dee saper ogni gran moda,
She must know for good or evil		Dove il diavolo ha la coda,
What the devil does with his tail;		Cosa è bene e mal cos'è;
If she knows the little catches		Dee saper le maliziette
Which a little experience teaches,		Che innamorano gli amanti:
By pretending and delighting,		Finger riso, finger pianti,
She will surely tame the male.		Inventar i bei perchè;
Modest and wary		Dee in momento
Yet all inviting,		Dar retta a cento;
Of favours chary		Colle pupille
Yet all delighting;		Parlar con mille;
All charms revealing,		Dar speme a tutti,
All heart concealing,		Sien belli o brutti;
Smiles must flow gushingly,		Saper nascondersi
Lies come unblushingly,		Senza confondersi;
Spare no expedient		Senza arrossire
To make obedient,		Saper mentire;
Handsome and comely,		E, qual regina
Ugly and homely,		Dall'alto soglio,
Anything else in the		Col 'posso e voglio'
Shape of a man.		Farsi ubbidir.

(*aside*)

Artful in scheming,	Par ch'abbian gusto
Artless in seeming,	Di tal dottrina.
Stooping to conquer	Viva Despina
Be ever her plan.	Che sa servir!
By arts alluring	Senza arrossire
Victims securing,	Saper mentire,

Queen of the nation	E, qual regina
Gracious and glorious,	Dall'alto soglio,
Ever victorious,	Col 'posso e voglio'
She wins the day.	Farsi ubbidir.

I see they're yielding,	Par ch'abbian gusto
By their demeanour,	Di tal dottrina.
Clever Despina,	Viva Despina
She knows the way.	Che sa servir!

(She leaves.)

Scene Two. *Fiordiligi and Dorabella. / Secco Recitative*

FIORDILIGI

Well, sister! What do you think?	Sorella, cosa dici?

DORABELLA

I am astounded;	Io son stordita
For a girl such ideas are simply dreadful.	Dallo spirto infernal di tal ragazza.

FIORDILIGI

She must be quite demented.	Ma, credimi: è un pazza.
As if she could persuade us	Ti par che siamo in caso
To adopt her suggestion.	Di seguir suoi consigli?

DORABELLA

Oh, quite out of the question	Oh, certo, se tu pigli
If you look at it that way.	Pel rovescio il negozio.

FIORDILIGI

What other way, dear,	Anzi, io lo piglio
Could it ever be looked at?	Per il suo verso dritto:
Do you believe it's proper	Non credi tu delitto,
For young ladies engaged to be married	Per due giovani omai promesse spose,
To follow her suggestion?	Il far di queste cose?

DORABELLA

Not really proper	Ella non dice
But I don't see the harm.	Che facciamo alcun mal.

FIORDILIGI

Think of the gossip!	È mal che basta
We'd never live it down.	Il far parlar di noi.

DORABELLA

That's not a problem,	Quando si dice
They come to see Despina.	Che vengon per Despina! . . .

FIORDILIGI

Oh, you've acquired	Oh, tu sei troppo
A latitude of conscience. What should we say	Larga di coscienza! E che diranno,
To our fiancés?	Gli sposi nostri?

DORABELLA

Nothing.	Nulla:
The affair will be over.	O non sapran l'affare,
They'll know nothing about it.	Ed è tutto finito;
There's no need to upset them. You know the proverb,	O sapran qualche cosa, e allor diremo
'Where ignorance is bliss'.	Che vennero per lei.

FIORDILIGI

And our devotion?	Ma i nostri cori?

Flows in the old direction;	Restano quel che sono:
We only seek diversion to ward off melancholy	Per divertirsi un poco e non morire
While they are absent.	Dalla malinconia,
There is nothing in that to be ashamed of.	Non si manca di fè, sorella mia.

FIORDILIGI

Very true!	Questo è ver.

DORABELLA

Well then?	Dunque?

FIORDILIGI

Well then,	Dunque,
As you will! But remember,	Fa' un po' tu; ma non voglio
I'm blameless if it brings complications.	Aver colpa, se poi nasce un imbroglio.

DORABELLA

With such careful precautions,	Che imbroglio nascer deve,
Could anything go wrong? Now for the strangers.	Con tanta precauzion? Per altro, ascolta:
There is one point unsettled —	Per intenderci bene,
To arrange how the spoil shall be divided.	Qual vuoi sceglier per te de' due narcisi?

FIORDILIGI

It's you who must decide, dear.	Decidi tu, sorella.

DORABELLA

I have decided.	Io già decisi:

No. 20 Duet

I prefer the rather dark one,	[10] Prenderò quel brunettino,
With the greater sense of fun.	Che più lepido mi par.

FIORDILIGI

Very well, I'll take the fair one	Ed intanto io col biondino
And the comedy's begun.	Vo' un po' ridere e burlar.

DORABELLA

To his words of ardent passion	Scherzosetta, ai dolci detti
Jokingly will I reply.	Io di quel risponderò.

FIORDILIGI

Sigh and glance in imitation	Sospirando, i sospiretti
I'll return for glance and sigh.	Io dell'altro imiterò.

DORABELLA

He will say, 'Behold my anguish!'	Mi dirà: 'Ben mio, mi moro!'

FIORDILIGI

He will say, 'For you I languish!'	Mi dirà: 'Mio bel tesoro!'

FIORDILIGI AND DORABELLA

We will pass the time in pleasure.	Ed intanto, che diletto,
With each other we will vie.	Che spassetto io proverò!

(As they leave, they meet Don Alfonso.)

Scene Three. *Fiordiligi, Dorabella and Don Alfonso. / Secco Recitative*

DON ALFONSO

Come at once to the garden.	Ah, correte al giardino,
You most fortunate ladies! It's amazing!	Le mie care ragazze! Che allegria!
Such instruments! Such music!	Che musica! che canto!
This is truly spectacular — enchanting!	Che brillante spettacolo! che incanto!
With a spell they'll surround you.	Fate presto, correte!

DORABELLA

Whatever can it be?   Che diamine esser può?

DON ALFONSO

Come, they'll astound you!   Tosto vedrete.

(*They leave.*)

Scene Four. *A garden by the sea-shore, with grassy seats and two stone tables. At the landing-place a boat adorned with flowers. Ferrando, Guglielmo, Dorabella, Fiordiligi, Despina, Don Alfonso, sailors and servants.*
  Ferrando and Guglielmo and a band of singers and musicians in the boat; Despina in the garden; Fiordiligi and Dorabella accompanied by Don Alfonso enter from one side: attendants in rich liveries receive them. / No. 21 Duet and Chorus

FERRANDO AND GUGLIELMO

Gentle zephyr, softly sighing,	Secondate, aurette amiche,
To the strains of love replying,	Secondate i miei desiri,
In the ear of yonder fair maiden	E portate i miei sospiri
All my whispered vows repeat!	Alla Dea di questo cor.
Take my kisses, breathe them o'er her,	Voi che udiste mille volte
Murmur low how I adore her!	Il tenor delle mie pene,
Take my tears, and with them laden	Ripetete al caro bene
Pour the offering at her feet.	Tutto quel che udiste allor.

CHORUS

Gentle zephyr, softly sighing,	Secondate, aurette amiche,
All my whispered vows repeat.	Il desir di si bei cor.

(*During the chorus, Ferrando and Guglielmo come off the boat with garlands of flowers. Don Alfonso and Despina accompany them to the ladies who are stunned into silence. / Secco Recitative*)

DON ALFONSO
(*to the servants, who are carrying baskets of flowers, etc.*)

Bring all the baskets here,	Il tutto deponete
And put them down on the table, then you get back	Sopra quei tavolini, e nella barca
Into the barge discreetly.	Ritiratevi, amici.

FIORDILIGI AND DORABELLA

What's all this masquerading?   Cos'è tal mascherata?

DESPINA
(*to Ferrando and Guglielmo*)

Now for your speech, take courage! Or have you lost	Animo, via, coraggio! Avete perso
The use of your tongues completely?	L'uso della favella?

(*The barge leaves the shore and disappears.*)

FERRANDO

I'm gasping, I'm trembling   Io tremo e palpito
And I'm shaking all over.   Dalla testa alle piante.

GUGLIELMO

My love ties up my legs, prevents me   Amor lega le membra a vero amante.
  moving.

DON ALFONSO
(*to the ladies*)

Do give them some encouragement.   Da brave, incoraggiateli!

FIORDILIGI
(*to the lovers*)

Good evening!   Parlate.

96

DORABELLA
(to the lovers)

Pray be at ease and speak your meaning freely.	Liberi dite pur quel che bramate.

FERRANDO

Dear lady.	Madama ...

GUGLIELMO

No, dearest ladies.	Anzi, madame ...

FERRANDO
(to Guglielmo)

Speak for us both.	Parla pur tu.

GUGLIELMO
(to Ferrando)

No, no, I'll second you.	No, no, parla pur tu.

DON ALFONSO

Oh, this is too ridiculous!	Oh, cospetto del diavolo!
Such ceremonious fashions	Lasciate tali smorfie
Belong to days gone by. Despinetta,	Del secolo passato. Despinetta,
We will end this indecision.	Terminiam questa festa:
You tutor her. I will take charge of this one.	Fa' tu con lei quel ch'io farò con questa.

No. 22 Quartet

(He takes Dorabella by the hand; Despina takes Fiordiligi's.)

Now give me your hand	La mano a me date,
Come forward a pace.	Movetevi un po'.

(to the lovers)

Since you will say nothing,	Se voi non parlate,
I'll speak in your place.	Per voi parlerò.

(to the ladies)

The humblest of slaves	Perdono vi chiede
Is imploring your pardon!	Un schiavo tremante:
His sorrow beholding,	V'offese, lo vede,
Your heart do not harden;	Ma solo un istante.
Oh light be his sentence!	Or pena, ma tace ...

FERRANDO AND GUGLIELMO
(repeating the last word in the same tone)

... Sentence! ...	... Tace ...

DON ALFONSO

... Nor doubt his repentance ...	... Or lasciavi in pace ...

FERRANDO AND GUGLIELMO
(as before)

... Repentance! ...	... In pace ...

DON ALFONSO

... If love cannot move you,	... Non può quel che vuole,
Compassion must try.	Vorrà quel che può.

FERRANDO AND GUGLIELMO
(repeating the last two lines, with a sigh)

... If love cannot move you	... Non può quel che vuole,
Compassion must try.	Vorrà quel che può.

DON ALFONSO
(to the ladies)

Still silent, did you hear me?	Su, via, rispondete!
You're staring and you're laughing.	Guardate ... e ridete?

DESPINA
(standing in front of the two ladies)

Then with your permission	Per voi la risposta
I'll give your reply.	A loro darò.

Past things are past undoing,	Quello ch'è stato è stato.
Old vows beyond renewing!	Scordiamci del passato:
Sever the bond for ever	Rompasi omai quel laccio
Symbol of servitude.	Segno di servitù.

(She takes Dorabella's hand, Don Alfonso takes Fiordiligi's: they break the garlands and they lace them around the arms of the lovers. Then to the lovers:)

Now take this hand in token	A me porgete il braccio,
The ice has now been broken,	Nè sospirate più,
Then sigh no more, I beg of you.	Nè sospirate più.

DESPINA AND DON ALFONSO
(to one side, sottovoce)

And now we must be going	Per carità, partiamo;
And leave them to their wooing.	Quel che san far veggiamo.
I'll wager with the Devil	Le stimo più del diavolo,
A surrender will ensue.	S'ora non cascan giù.

(They leave.)

Scene Five. *Fiordiligi, Dorabella, Ferrando and Guglielmo. Dorabella on Guglielmo's arm; Fiordiligi with Ferrando, without giving him her arm. They make a little silent scene, gazing at each other, sighing, laughing, etc. / Secco Recitative*

FIORDILIGI

Isn't the weather lovely!	Oh, che bella giornata!

FERRANDO

I find it rather too warm.	Caldetta anzichè no.

DORABELLA

Oh, how lovely the trees are!	Che vezzosi arboscelli!

GUGLIELMO

Very lovely! But alas	Certo, certo, son belli:
It seems there's far more leaf than fruit.	Han più foglie che frutti.

FIORDILIGI

	It is cooler		Quei viali
In the shade of the pine trees.		Come sono leggiadri!	
Pray let me take your arm!		Volete passeggiar?	

FERRANDO

	With greatest pleasure,		Son pronto, o cara,
Your wish is my commandment.		Ad ogni vostro cenno.	

FIORDILIGI

	You're too civil.	Troppa grazia!

FERRANDO
(sottovoce, as he passes Guglielmo)

Now for the fateful moment.	Eccoci alla gran crisi.

FIORDILIGI

What was your observation?	Cosa gli avete detto?

FERRANDO

Just a recommendation	Eh, gli raccomandai
To follow our example.	Di divertirla bene.

(*to Guglielmo*)

Shall we too take a stroll?	Passeggiamo anche noi.

GUGLIELMO

Only too pleased to.	Come vi piace.

(*They stroll on. After a moment of silence . . .*)

Oh, dear!	Ahimè!

DORABELLA

I beg your pardon?	Che cosa avete?

GUGLIELMO

There's a feeling inside me,	Io mi sento sì male,
An awful desperate feeling.	Sì male, anima mia,
I'm afraid it will kill me.	Che mi par di morire.

(*The others continue their scene silently in the distance.*)

DORABELLA
(*aside*)

I'm not the least surprised at it.	Non otterrà nientissimo.

(*to Guglielmo*)

Perhaps you've not recovered	Saranno rimasugli
From the poison you swallowed.	Del velen che beveste.

GUGLIELMO
(*with excitement*)

Ah, but the poison had an essence	Ah, che un veleno assai più forte io bevo
(if you'll excuse	
My boldness) which is kindled	In que' crudi e focosi
Into fire by your presence!	Mongibelli amorosi!

(*The others stroll off-stage.*)

DORABELLA

Why, then the safest remedy	Sarà veleno calido:
Is to apply cold water.	Fatevi un poco fresco.

GUGLIELMO

Your jest makes pain more painful	Ingrata, voi burlate,
When your kindness might cure it!	Ed intanto io mi moro!

(*aside*)

They have left us!	Son spariti:
Where on earth have they gone to?	Dove diamin son iti?

DORABELLA

Better endure it!	Eh, via, non fate . . .

GUGLIELMO

I am dying and meanwhile you only	Io mi moro, crudele, e voi burlate?
mock me.	

DORABELLA

I mock you? I mock you?	Io burlo? io burlo?

GUGLIELMO

Can I doubt it?	Dunque,
Unless you grant me one little token	Datemi qualche segno, anima bella,
Ere you bid me depart!	Della vostra pietà.

DORABELLA

Two, if you want them!	Due, se volete:
When your wishes are spoken, I will grant them.	Dite quel che far deggio, e lo vedrete.

GUGLIELMO
(aside)

Really, or is she still joking?
(to Dorabella, showing her a pendant in the shape of a heart)
This is merely a token,
Will you deign to accept it?

Scherza, o dice davvero?

Questa picciola offerta
D'accettare degnatevi.

DORABELLA

A token?

Un core?

FERRANDO

A symbol to represent the heart
Which beats in my bosom, which beats for
   you alone!

Un core: è simbolo di quello
Ch'arde, languisce e spasima per voi.

DORABELLA
(aside)

A wonderful present.

Che dono prezioso.

GUGLIELMO

Will you wear it?

L'accettate?

DORABELLA

I must not.
You'd attempt to seduce an honest woman.

Crudele!
Di sedur non tentate un cor fedele.

GUGLIELMO
(aside)

Like a fortress on quicksands!
I'd spare her but I've given
The oath of a soldier.

La montagna vacilla.
Mi spiace: ma impegnato
È l'onor di soldato.
(to Dorabella)

I love you!

V'adoro!

DORABELLA

Oh, for shame!

Per pietà ...

GUGLIELMO

No, I adore you!

Son tutto vostro!

DORABELLA

No, really!

Oh, Dei!

GUGLIELMO

Do you reproach me?

Cedete, o cara!

DORABELLA

I am greatly to blame.

Mi farete morir ...

GUGLIELMO

The blame is equal
If you're willing to share it.
You will wear it?

Morremo insieme,
Amorosa mia speme.
L'accettate?

DORABELLA
(after a moment, with a sigh)

I'll wear it!

L'accetto.

GUGLIELMO
(aside)

Oh, forgive me, Ferrando!
(to Dorabella)
Let me declare it!

Infelice Ferrando!

Oh, che diletto!

This heart that I give you	[11] Il core vi dono,
I pray you to treasure,	Bell'idolo mio.
And yours in return, love,	Ma il vostro vo' anch'io:
Oh, render to me.	Via, datelo a me.

DORABELLA

The heart that you give me	Mel date, lo prendo;
I take it with pleasure,	Ma il mio non vi rendo.
But that which you ask for ...	Invan mel chiedete:
No longer is free.	Più meco ei non è.

GUGLIELMO

Oh, do not deceive me!	Se teco non l'hai
What beating is here?	Perchè batte qui?

DORABELLA

And if yours you have given	Se a me tu lo dai,
What throbbing is there?	Che mai balza li?

DORABELLA AND GUGLIELMO

The heart that was mine, love,	È il mio coricino
For you now is beating,	Che più non è meco:
To you is repeating	Ei venne a star teco,
A message of love.	Ei batte cosi.

GUGLIEMO
(He tries to exchange her miniature for his pendant.)

With you let me leave it.	Qui lascia che il metta.

DORABELLA

No, that may not be.	E qui non può star.

GUGLIEMO

Oh come now, receive it.	T'intendo, furbetta.

DORABELLA

How dare you!	Che fai?

GUGLIELMO

Shut your eyes.	Non guardar.

(He turns her face gently to one side, removes the miniature and replaces it with the pendant.)

DORABELLA
(aside)

I feel a Vesuvius	Nel petto un Vesuvio
Erupting inside.	D'avere mi par.

GUGLIELMO
(aside)

Ferrando forgive me.	Ferrando meschino!
How shall I confide?	Possibil non par.

(to Dorabella)

Your eyes you may open.	L'occhietto a me gira.

DORABELLA

What folly!	Che brami?

GUGLIELMO

Admire it,	Rimira
Resistance is vain.	Se meglio può andar.

DORABELLA AND FERRANDO

Oh happy communion	Oh, cambio felice
Of new love requiting,	Di cori e d'affetti!

| To pleasure inviting, | Che nuovi diletti, |
| What exquisite pain! | Che dolce penar! |

(They leave with their arms around each other.)

Scene Six. *Fiordiligi and Ferrando. Fiordiligi enters in agitation, followed by Ferrando. / Accompanied Recitative*

FERRANDO

| Cruel one, would you leave me? | Barbara, perchè fuggi? |

FIORDILIGI

| I flee a basilisk, | Ho visto un aspide, |
| A hydra, a vicious scorpion. | Un'idra, un basilisco! |

FERRANDO

All too clear is your answer.	Ah, crudel, ti capisco!
Basilisk, hydra and vicious scorpion and, if there be	L'aspide, l'idra, il basilisco, e quanto
In Libyan desert monster more appalling,	I libici deserti han di più fiero,
Then to that you'd compare me.	In me solo tu vedi.

FIORDILIGI

| I know it, I know it. | È vero, è vero. |
| You destroy my composure. | Tu vuoi tormi la pace. |

FERRANDO

| To replace it with rapture. | Ma per farti felice. |

FIORDILIGI

| That way you only harm me. | Cessa di molestarmi! |

FERRANDO

| Just one glance will suffice me. | Non ti chiedo che un guardo. |

FIORDILIGI

| Leave me! | Partiti! |

FERRANDO

I refuse to,	Non sperarlo,
Till those proud eyes command me to obey you.	Se pria gli occhi men fieri a me non giri.
Oh Heaven! That look was tender, those sighs betray you.	O ciel, ma tu mi guardi e poi sospiri?

No. 24 Aria*
(very happily)

Well I knew that a spirit of beauty	Ah, lo veggio: quell'anima bella
All my pleading could never deny,	Al mio pianto resister non sa;
Or if torn between passion and duty	Non è fatta per esser rubella
Her affection could never defy.	Agli affetti di amica pietà.

By those glances, by the breath of your sighing,	In quel guardo, in quei cari sospiri
Your affection enkindles my heart.	Dolce raggio lampeggia al mio cor:
As a flower to the sun ever turning,	Già rispondi a' miei caldi desiri,
Blooms my love in the light of your eyes!	Già tu cedi al più tenero amor.

(sadly)

| But you spurn me, you spurn me, hard-hearted! | Ma tu fuggi, spietata, tu taci |
| To my plea will you give no reply? | Ed invano mi senti languir? |

| Ah, how quickly is fond hope departed! | Ah, cessate, speranze fallaci: |
| She condemns me to languish and die. | La crudel mi condanna a morir. |

(He leaves.)

---

* This aria is often ommitted in performance.

Scene Seven. *Fiordiligi alone. / Accompanied Recitative*

FIORDILIGI

He's left me. Listen! . . . Ah no! No, let him leave me!
So hastens from my presence the fatal object
Of my weakness and folly. Ah, what a torment,
I suffer in his presence . . . A just affliction,
I deserve all my anguish. At such a moment,
How could I dare give audience
To the passions of this man? To treat with jesting
An intention so serious? Oh, my beloved,
You'd be right to condemn me, leave me for ever.
This passion, this sudden burning in my senses
Is no blameless affliction: it's madness, and weakness,
Confusion, void of reason,
Fatal error! It's falsehood and treason!

Ei parte . . . Senti! . . . Ah, no: partir si lasci,
Si tolga ai sguardi miei l'infausto oggetto
Della mia debolezza. A qual cimento
Il barbaro mi pose . . . Un premio è questo
Ben dovuto a mie colpe! In tale istante
Dovea di nuovo amante
I sospiri ascoltar? l'altrui querele
Dovea volger in gioco? Ah, questo core
A ragione condanni, o giusto amore!
Io ardo; e l'ardor mio non è più effetto
D'un amor virtuoso: è smania, affanno
Rimorso, pentimento,
Leggerezza, perfidia e tradimento!

No. 25 Rondò

Ah, my love, I pray forgiveness [12]
For the wrong my soul has harboured.
'Neath these branches, among these shadows,
I will hide it for evermore.

I will purge this base emotion
With my love and my devotion.
I will banish the dread remembrance
Which with horror shames my heart.

Ah, my love so true! So tender!
What have I to give you now?
For your love I can but render
Faithless heart and broken vow.

Per pietà, ben mio, perdona
All'error d'un'alma amante:
Fra quest'ombre e queste piante
Sempre ascoso, oh, Dio, sarà!

Svenerà quest' empia voglia
L'ardir mio, la mia costanza
Perderà la rimembranza
Che vergogna e orror mi fa.

A chi mai mancò di fede
Questo vano, ingrato cor!
Si dovea miglior mercede,
Caro bene, al tuo candor.

(*She leaves.*)

Scene Eight. *Ferrando and Guglielmo. / Secco Recitative*

FERRANDO
(*very happily*)

We've done it! Poor Don Alfonso!

Amico, abbiamo vinto!

GUGLIELMO

A skirmish? An ambush?

Un ambo, o un terno?

FERRANDO

Neither. A total victory! Fiordiligi
Is modesty incarnate.

Una cinquina, amico: Fiordiligi
È la modestia in carne.

GUGLIELMO

Are you certain?

Niente meno?

FERRANDO

No doubt of it, I'll tell you
Exactly what occurred.

Nientissimo. Sta' attento
E ascolta come fu.

GUGLIELMO

I would not miss a word.

T'ascolto: di' pur su.

103

FERRANDO

After we left you,	Pel giardinetto,
Once out of sight securely,	Come eravam s'accordo,
I gave my hand politely;	A passeggiar mi metto;
She accepted demurely.	Le dò il braccio; si parla
The conversation flowed on brightly	Di mille cose indifferenti; alfine
Until I came to the point.	Viensi all'amor.

GUGLIELMO

Oh, did you?	Avanti.

FERRANDO

Choked with sobs I protested,	Fingo labbra tremanti,
'Love unrequited racks my	Fingo di pianger, fingo
Very soul out of joint!'	Di morir al suo piè.

GUGLIELMO

Pretty strong for a start!	Bravo assai, per mia fè.
And she said . . .?	Ed ella?

FERRANDO

Laughed at my words	Ella da prima
To start with, mocked them, dismissed them.	Ride, scherza, mi burla.

GUGLIELMO

And then?	E poi?

FERRANDO

Then I	E poi
Said she must kill or cure me.	Finge d'impietosirsi.

GUGLIELMO

What a performance!	Oh, cospettaccio!

FERRANDO

And then came the explosion!	Alfin scoppia la bomba.
She's as chaste as a lily	Pura come colomba
And as true to Guglielmo as any compass.	Al suo caro Guglielmo ella si serba:
She dismissed me with outrage.	Mi discaccia superba.
She reviled me, abused me,	Mi maltratta, mi fugge,
Giving positive evidence in this manner	Testimonio rendendomi e messaggio
That with pride you can be sure of her honour.	Che una femmina ell'è senza paraggio.

GUGLIELMO

Bravo you! Bravo me!	Bravo tu, bravo io,
Brava my true Penelope!	Brava la mia Penelope!
Come and let me embrace you	Lascia un po' ch'io tu abbracci
For such wonderful tidings.	Per si felice augurio,
O most welcome messenger!	O mio fido Mercurio!

(*They embrace.*)

FERRANDO

Now for my Dorabella,	E la mia Dorabella?
Did she refuse your wooing?	Come s'è diportata?

(*with rapture*)

How could I ever doubt it? I need no answer,	Oh, non ci ho neppur dubbio! assai conosco
Knowing how much she loves me!	Quella sensibil alma.

GUGLIELMO

A perfect picture	Eppur, un dubbio,
Is apt to prove deceptive.	Parlandoti a quattr'occhi,
It may not be as real as you thought it!	Non saria mal, se tu l'avessi!

FERRANDO

What's that?   Come?

GUGLIELMO

Portraits can be unreal.   Dico cosi per dir.
(aside)
          The dose is bitter,   Avrei piacere
So the pill must be sugared.   D'indorargli la pillola.

FERRANDO

Speak man! Are you suggesting   Stelle! Cesse ella forse
Dorabella is faithless? Have you succeeded?   Alle lusinghe tue? Ah, s'io potessi
Are you trying to provoke me?   Sospettarlo soltanto!

GUGLIELMO

          To be romantic   È sempre bene
Scarcely befits the world that we inhabit.   Il sospettare un poco, in questo mondo.

FERRANDO

Some sort of riddle! Explain it! Are you   Eterni Dei, favella! A fuoco lento
  suggesting
Dorabella is false? But no, you're joking!   Non mi far qui morir . . . Ma no, tu vuoi
Doing her an injustice. Nothing could   Prenderti meco spasso; ella non ama,
  injure
Her devotion to me.   Non adora che me.

GUGLIELMO

          Clearly! A devotion   Certo! Anzi, in prova
So intense that, to show it,   Di suo amor, di sua fede,
Here is the proof she gave me, do you know   Questo bel ritrattino ella mi diede.
  it?

(He shows him the miniature that Dorabella has given him.)

FERRANDO
(furiously)

Gave you my portrait!   Il mio ritratto!

Accompanied Recitative

    Ah, perfidy!   Ah, perfida!
        (as though leaving)

GUGLIELMO

Where are you going?   Ove vai?

FERRANDO

To tear the heart out of her faithless bosom   A trarle il cor dal scellerato petto
        (furiously)
And to avenge love and devotion slighted.   E a vendicar il mio tradito affetto.

GUGLIELMO

Calm yourself!   Fermati!

FERRANDO
(resolutely)

    No, release me!   No, mi lascia!

GUGLIELMO

          Are you raving?   Sei tu pazzo?
Will you indeed abandon yourself   Vuoi tu precipitarti
To ruin for a worthless woman?   Per una donna che non val due soldi?
Don't let woman's folly   Non vorrei che facesse
Drive you to desperation.   Qualche corbelleria.

FERRANDO

Traitress! Such protestations   Numi! Tante promesse,

And promises, tender glances and fond
embraces
In a moment forgotten
As a vision of night!

E lagrime, e sospiri, e giuramenti,
In sì pochi momenti
Come l'empia oblìo?

GUGLIELMO

Don't ask me to explain.

Perbacco, io non lo so.

FERRANDO

Who can I turn to?
Where can I go now? What aim in life is left
me?
Pity a broken heart, grant me your guidance.

Che fare or deggio?
A qual partito, a qual idea m'appiglio?

Abbi di mi pietà: dammi consiglio.

GUGLIELMO

My friend I must admit
I've no guidance to give!

Amico, non saprei
Qual consiglio a te dar.

FERRANDO

Treacherous and heartless!
Scarce a day had I left her!

Barbara! ingrata!
In un giorno!... in poche ore!...

GUGLIELMO

It's a more wicked world than we had
dreamed of!

Certo, un caso quest'è da far stupore.

No. 26 Aria

Ladies have such variations,
Permutations, complications,
That to hear the mournful tale
Of a lover's provocations
Well might make the cheek grow pale!

[13]

Donne mie, la fate a tanti
E tanti, a tanti e tanti,
Che, se il ver vi deggio dir,
Se si lagnano gli amanti,
Li comincio a compatir.

Charming creatures! We adore them!
And they know it! Far, far too well!
Every day we bow before them,
Nor against their power rebel!
But, alas, their vacillations, fluctuations,
Are enough to break the spell!

Io vo' bene al sesso vostro,
Lo sapete, ognun lo sa:
Ogni giorno ve lo mostro,
Vi dò segno d'amistà;
Ma quel farla a tanti e tanti
M'avvilisce, in verità.

Bravely soldiers may protect them,
Sailors guard the seas afar,
Priests may counsel and direct them,
Lawyers argue at the Bar –
Yet the ladies' retractations, abjurations,
Baffle men of peace and war!

Mille volte il brando presi
Per salvar il vostro onor,
Mille volte vi difesi
Colla bocca e più col cor;
Ma quel farla a tanti e tanti
È un vizietto seccator.

Lovely forms and charming faces!
Nature, in her kindly plan,
Dowered them lavishly with graces,
Ever since the world began;
But, the ladies' aberrations,
Hesitations,
Mystify the doting man!
But what feminine evasions,
And mental reservations,
O naughty, flighty,
Pretty, petty ladies!
When you talk of love's vexations
All my pity's for the man!

Siete vaghe, siete amabili,
Più tesori il ciel vi diè,
E le grazie vi circondano
Dalla testa sino ai piè;
Ma la fate a tanti e tanti,
A tanti e tanti,
Che credibile non è.
Ma la fate a tanti e tanti,
A tanti e tanti,
A tanti e tanti,
A tanti e tanti,
Che, se gridano gli amanti,
Hanno certo un gran perchè.

Scene Nine. *Ferrando, then Guglielmo and Don Alfonso. / Accompanied Recitative*

FERRANDO

Ah! My brain is distracted! The voice of
reason
Is overwhelmed by the conflicting urges of
passion!

In qual fiero contrasto, in qual disordine

Di pensieri e di affetti io mi ritrovo?

So completely unheard of is my dilemma,	Tanto insolito e novo è il caso mio,
That there's no one, but no one,	Che non altri, non io
Competent to advise me . . . Alfonso, Alfonso,	Basto per consigliarmi . . . Alfonso, Alfonso,
What contempt you will feel	Quanto rider vorrai
For my naive behaviour!	Della mia stupidezza!
But I shall be avenged! You faithless woman!	Ma mi vendicherò: saprò dal seno
You will see from now onwards	Cancellar quell'iniqua,
With scorn I'll dismiss you . . .	Saprò, cancellarla . . .

I'll dismiss you?	Cancellarla?
Vain attempt if my heart fails to resist you.	Troppo, odio, questio cor per lei mi parla.

(Don Alfonso meets Guglielmo and stays to listen.)

No. 27 Cavatina*

Her treason is poison	[14]	Tradito, schernito
That tortures my heart.		Dal perfido cor,
Though her love may falter,		Io sento che ancora
Yet mine cannot alter,		Quest'alma l'adora,
I still hear the accents		Io sento per essa
Of love in my heart!		Le voci d'amor.

† *Secco Recitative*

DON ALFONSO
(approaching Ferrando)

Bravo! That does you credit!	Bravo! Questa è costanza!

FERRANDO

Oh you barbarian,	Andate, o barbaro!
It's to you I'm indebted!	Per voi misero sono.

DON ALFONSO

It is a trying situation	Via, se sarete buono
But I'm sure you'll soon recover. Now listen!	Vi tornerò l'antica calma. Udite:

(indicating Guglielmo)

Fiordiligi at this stage	Fiordiligi a Guglielmo
To Guglielmo is true, but Dorabella	Si conserva fedel, a Dorabella
Has been less so to you.	Infedel a voi fu.

FERRANDO

She has disgraced me.	Per mia vergogna.

GUGLIELMO

Dear Ferrando! There is a	Caro amico, bisogna
Difference which perhaps may have escaped you.	Far delle differenze in ogni cosa:
Had Nature only made me	Ti pare che una sposa
A little less attractive (it isn't vanity,	Mancar possa a un Guglielmo? Un picciol calcolo,
I only speak from hearsay)	Non parlo per lodarmi
Then your bet would be won. But Dorabella	Se facciamo tra noi . . . Tu vedi, amico
Was overwhelmed by Nature.	Che un poco più di merto . . .

DON ALFONSO

You must admit it.	Eh, anch'io lo dico.

GUGLIELMO

But Fiordiligi's steadfast.	Intanto mi darete
You owe me fifty guineas.	Cinquanta zecchinetti.

---

*This cavatina is often cut in performance.

† This recitative is often shortened in performance.

DON ALFONSO

Just a moment.	Volontieri.
First the terms of the bet must be completed	Pria però di pagar, vo' che facciamo
Lest either be cheated.	Qualche altra esperienza.

GUGLIELMO

Cheated?	Come?

DON ALFONSO

The chances are even: you're winning so far,	Abbiate pazienza; infin domani
But I have till tomorrow. I must remind you	Siete entrambi miei schiavi: a me voi deste
You have to do my bidding	Parola da soldati
And the oath you have sworn, remember, must last till the time is up.	Di far quel ch'io dirò. Venite: io spero
'By all means boast	
About your eggs	Mostrarvi ben che folle è quel cervello
But before they are hatched	
Don't count your chickens.'	Che sulla frasca ancor vende l'uccello.*

(*They leave.*)

Scene Ten. *A room with several doors, little tables and a mirror. Dorabella and Despina; then Fiordiligi.*

DESPINA

Now at last you are acting	Ora vedo che siete
As a sane woman should do!	Una donna di garbo.

DORABELLA

Indeed, Despina,	Invan, Despina,
I resisted in vain. The wicked wretch	Di resister tentai: quel demonietto
So hotly pursued me, I had to listen. He wooed me	Ha un artifizio, un'eloquenza, un tratto
With a fire that would melt a heart of stone.	Che ti fa cader giù se sei di sasso.

DESPINA†

Hot as a little demon!	Corpo di satanasso,
Seems you have found a man who has discovered	Questo vuol dir saper! Tanto di raro
The way to woo a woman.	Noi povere ragazze
The odds are so against it	Abbiamo in po' di bene.
You can truly be thankful you're so lucky.	Che bisogna pigliarlo, allor ch'ei viene.

(*Fiordiligi enters.*)

Oh goodness, here's your sister –	Ma ecco la sorella.
And furious!	Che ceffo!

FIORDILIGI

Oh, you wretches!	Sciagurate!
It is entirely your fault	Ecco per colpa vostra
That it's turned out so badly.	In che stato mi trovo!

DESPINA

What's the matter?	Cosa è nato,
Why are you taking on so?	Cara madamigella?

DORABELLA

Has anything distressed you?	Hai qualche mal, sorella?

FIORDILIGI

The Devil take us all,	Ho il diavolo che porti

---

* Literally: Come: I hope to show you clearly how foolish is the mind that sells the bird which is still on the bough.

† These five lines are often cut, as are several other passages in this scene.

Myself, you, you too, Don Alfonso, those evil strangers And every soul in creation!	Me, te, lei, Don Alfonso, i forastieri E quanti pazzi ha il mondo!

DORABELLA

Are you out of your senses?	Hai perduto il giudizio?

FIORDILIGI

Worse than madness, Total disaster. I'm in love, and yet I know My love is not only for Guglielmo!	Peggio, peggio . . . Inorridisci: io amo! e l'amor mio Non è sol per Guglielmo.

DESPINA

Frank admission!	Meglio, meglio!

DORABELLA

(Was there ever so neat a turn as this?) Is the other 'the fair one'?	E che sì, che anche tu se' innamorata Del galante biondino?

FIORDILIGI
(sighing)

Yes, I own it with shame.	Ah, purtroppo per noi!

DESPINA

That's perfect.	Ma brava!

DORABELLA

Darling, A hundred thousand kisses! Yours the fair one, mine the dark one: Let's have a double wedding.	Tieni Settantamila baci, Tu il biondino, io 'l brunetto: Eccoci entrambe spose!

FIORDILIGI

What are you saying? Have you no pang of conscience, No concern, no remorse? Our poor fiancés Have departed in grief this very morning. Your barbarity shocks me. Where on earth did you learn it? It's not like you at all. How can you do it?	Cosa dici? Non pensi agli infelici Che stamane partir? Ai loro pianti, Alla lor fedeltà tu più non pensi? Così barbari sensi Dove, dove apprendesti? Sì diversa da te come ti festi?

DORABELLA

Listen dear. If they fight, And the fortunes of battle Should of our loves deprive us, consider (Is it not worth a thought?) Where are we should we survive them? With a prospect so appalling Who'll blame us for our actions?	* Odimi: sei tu certa Che non muoiano in guerra, I nostri vecchi amanti? E allora entrambe Resterem colle man piene di mosche. Tra un ben certo e un incerto C'è sempre un gran divario!

FIORDILIGI

Should they come back to claim us?	E se poi torneranno?

DORABELLA

If they survive they're lucky. We shall by then be married and I'm sure in A very distant country.	Se torneran, lor danno! Noi saremo allor mogli, noi saremo Lontane mille miglia.

FIORDILIGI

I don't see how the dictates Of the heart can change in one short evening.	Ma non so come mai Si può cangiar in un sol giorno un core.

---

* Often cut in performance.

DORABELLA

Now you're being ridiculous. We're women!	Che domanda ridicola! Siam donne!
And our nature decrees it.	E poi, tu com'hai fatto?

FIORDILIGI

I'll give the lie to that.	Io saprò vincermi.

DESPINA

You'll give the lie to no-one.	Voi non saprete nulla.

FIORDILIGI

You'll see that I'm in earnest.	Farò che tu lo veda.

DORABELLA

In our condition it's better to be honest.	Credi, sorella, è meglio che tu ceda.

No. 28 Aria

Young love is unrelenting,	[15]	È amore un ladroncello,
A serpent full of wiles,		Un serpentello è amor.
While lovers are lamenting,		Ei toglie e dà la pace,
Love only nods and smiles!		Come gli piace, ai cor.
He comes all unassuming,		Per gli occhi ai seno appena
But makes the heart a slave,		Un varco aprir si fa,
Then on his power presuming,		Che l'anima incatena
Takes back the joy he gave!		E toglie libertà.
Full of a sweet contentment		Porta dolcezza e gusto,
If you his rule obey,		Se tu lo lasci far;
But bitter his resentment		Ma t'empie di disgusto,
If you dispute his sway.		Se tenti di pugnar.
Nothing can you deny him,		Se nel tuo petto ei siede,
Whate'er he bids you do,		S'egli ti becca qui,
It's folly to defy him:		Fa' tutto quel ch'ei chiede,
And you will find it so!		Che anch'io farò così.

(*Dorabella and Despina leave.*)

Scene Eleven. *Fiordiligi alone; then Ferrando, Guglielmo and Don Alfonso in another room; later Despina. / Secco Recitative*

FIORDILIGI

All the world is conspiring	Come tutto congiura
To compel me to yield. But no, I'll perish	A sedurre il mio cor! Ma no! Si mora
Before complying! How could I be so weak	E non si ceda! Errai, quando alla suora
As to disclose it, and even to a servant?	Io mi scopersi ed alla serva mia:
She'll report my confession; if once he knows it	Esse a lui diran tutto, ed ei, più audace,
There's an end of resistance. Secure at home here	Fia di tutto capace . . . Agli occhi miei
I'll keep him at a distance; I'll tell Despina,	Mai più non comparisca: a tutti i servi

(*Ferrando, Guglielmo and Don Alfonso are seen through the open door, watching her from the next room.*)

Should he come here again,	Minaccerò il congedo,
She must show him the door. Such a seducer	Se lo lascian passar: veder nol voglio,
Must keep away.	Quel seduttor.

GUGLIELMO
(*to his friends*)

Bravissima!	Bravissima!
She is as chaste as Diana. Did you hear her?	La mia casta Artemisia! La sentite?

FIORDILIGI

Could I trust Dorabella?	Ma potria Dorabella,

110

No, I have cause to doubt her. Softly, what a notion!
Or does folly possess me? If I could dare it,
The uniforms would serve us
Which our lovers left behind them ...
  They shall! Despina!
Despina!

Senza saputa mia ... Piano! un pensiero
Per la mente mi passa: in casa mia
Restar molte uniformi
Di Guglielmo e di Ferrando ... Ardir!
  Despina!
Despina!

DESPINA
(entering)

Did you call?

Cosa c'è?

FIORDILIGI

Go at once to my dressing room, ask no questions,
Take the key of the wardrobe,
Forage behind the dresses and bring me quickly
The sabres and the helmets and both the cloaks
Which you will find there.

Tieni un po' questa chiave, e senza replica,
Senza replica alcuna,
Preni nel guardaroba e qui mi porta
Due spade, due cappelli e due vestiti
De' nostri sposi.

DESPINA

What do you think of doing?

E che volete fare?

FIORDILIGI

Go on and don't ask questions!

Vanne: non replicare!

DESPINA
(aside)

Well, what a way to talk, Miss High and Mighty!

Comanda in *abrégé*, Donna Arroganza!

(She leaves.)

FIORDILIGI

It's the last chance. Will it fail us?
If only Dorabella
Will follow my example, we'll join them as soldiers.
It's the only way left us
To escape from temptation.

Non c'è altro: ho speranza
Che Dorabella stessa
Seguirà il bell'esempio. Al campo! al campo!
Altra strada non resta,
Per serbarci innocenti.

DON ALFONSO
(aside)

Oh I see what she's up to!
(Re-enter Despina with the uniforms.)
Go ahead and seize your chance.

Ho capito abbastanza.

Vanne pur, non temer.

DESPINA
(to Fiordiligi)

Here they are.

Eccomi.

FIORDILIGI

    Now then,
Have some post-horses ordered,
Let them wait at the gate. Tell Dorabella that
I'll talk to her here.

    Vanne.
Sei cavalli di posta
Voli un servo a ordinar. Di' a Dorabella
Che parlar le vorrei.

DESPINA

Oh, very well, Miss.
(aside)
But I really believe she's going crazy.

Sarà servita.

Questa donna mi par di senno uscita.

(She leaves.)

111

Scene Twelve. *Fiordiligi; later Ferrando. Guglielmo and Don Alfonso in the other room.*

FIORDILIGI

This is Ferrando's helmet,	L'abito di Ferrando
It's exactly my size, and Guglielmo's	Sarà buono per me; può Dorabella
Will suffice Dorabella. None will suspect us	Prender quel di Guglielmo. In questi arnesi
And battle's fury not affright us. We'll join	Raggiungerem gli sposi nostri: al loro
Our lovers, all danger scorning,	Fianco pugnar potremo,
Until death can unite us.	E morir, se fa d'uopo.

(tearing off her head-dress)

Badge of my bondage,	Ite in malora,
With contempt I regard you! Thus I discard you.	Ornamenti fatali! Io vi detesto.

GUGLIELMO
(to his friends)

After that, of your charge freely acquit her!	Si può dar un amor simile a questo?

FIORDILIGI

Till the yoke of my true love safely has bound me	Di tornar non sperate alla mia fronte
No more my head shall you adorn; a headpiece	Pria ch'io qui torni col mio ben; in vostro
Fitter, with foes lurking around me, is this	Loco porrò questo cappello. Oh, come
A hero has worn. Does it suit me? Precisely!	Ei mi trasforma le sembianze e il viso!
And it sets off my style of beauty so nicely!	Come appena io medesma or mi ravviso!

No. 29 Duet

All too slowly the hours are fleeting,	[16]	Fra gli amplessi in pochi istanti
Till that happy hour of meeting;		Giungerò del fido sposo:
Thus arrayed, all danger scorning,		Sconosciuta, a lui davanti
To my lover's arms I'll fly.		In quest'abito verrò.
To his beating heart he'll press me,		Oh, che gioia il suo bel core
And with tender joy caress me.		Proverà nel ravvisarmi!

FERRANDO
(to Fiordiligi, as he enters)

While, alas your absence mourning,	Ed intanto di dolore,
I am left alone to die.	Meschinello, io mi morrò.

FIORDILIGI

Do not taunt me, I implore you.	Cosa veggio! Son tradita.
Leave, ah, leave me!	Deh, partite!

FERRANDO

Ah, I adore you!	Ah, no, mia vita!

(He takes his sword from the table and unsheathes it, etc..)

If my very presence pain you,	Con quel ferro di tua mano
If I have no hope to gain you,	Questo cor tu ferirai;
This alone I pray you grant me,	E se forza, oddio, non hai,
Now by this dear hand to die.	Io la man ti reggerò.

(He falls on his knees.)

FIORDILIGI

Silence! No more! Why do you haunt me?	Taci, ahimè! Son abbastanza
Will you with my folly taunt me?	Tormentata ed infelice!

FIORDILIGI AND FERRANDO
(aside)

Ah, I { feel my / see her } courage failing,	Ah, che omai la { mia / sua } costanza,
Tears like { mine / hers } are all availing	A quei sguardi, a quel che dice,

{ With a tender heart like mine.
{ Just one word and she is mine.

Incomincia a vacillar.

FIORDILIGI

Leave, ah, leave me!

Sorgi, sorgi!

FERRANDO

Then all is over.

Invan lo credi.

FIORDILIGI

What on earth can you be asking?

Per pietà, da me che chiedi?

FERRANDO

End my pain, or my existence.

Il tuo cor, o la mia morte.

FIORDILIGI

To his prayer there's no resistance!

Ah, non son, non son più forte . . .

FERRANDO

Don't reject me!

Cedi, cara!

(*He takes her hand and kisses it.*)

FIORDILIGI

Heaven direct me!

Dei, consiglio!

FERRANDO

Turn away your gaze no longer,
See in me a faithful suitor,
Husband or lover, whate'er you grant me.
        (*very tenderly*)
Be my love, do not refuse!

Volgi a me pietoso il ciglio:
In me sol trovar tu puoi
Sposo, amante . . . e più, se vuoi.
Idol mio, più no tardar.

FIORDILIGI
(*trembling*)

Ah, my heart, oh God, I'm vanquished:
Say no more for I am yours.

Giusto ciel! Crudel, hai vinto:
Fa' di me quel che ti par.

(*Don Alfonso restrains Guglielmo from bursting in.*)

FIORDILIGI AND FERRANDO

Now together, by love united,
Life shall seem no longer blighted.
Sorrow past shall be requited
With delight and joy divine.

Abbracciamci, o caro bene,
E un conforto a tante pene
Sia languir di dolce affetto
Di diletto sospirar.

(*They leave.*)

Scene Thirteen. *Guglielmo and Don Alfonso; then Ferrando. / Secco Recitative*

GUGLIELMO
(*entering with Don Alfonso*)

That is enough for me! Have I been dreaming?
How did I ever trust her?

Oh poveretto me! Cosa ho veduto,
Cosa ho sentito mai!

DON ALFONSO

For pity's sake be quiet!

Per carità, silenzio!

GUGLIELMO

I'd rather have the torment
Of red-hot pincers tearing,
Or leap into that volcano's crater!
Can that be Fiordiligi, my Penelope,
The Diana of chastity? Dissembler,
Double-dealer, impostor, serpent, traitress!

Mi pelerei la barba,
Mi graffierei la pelle,
E darei colle corna entro le stelle!
Fu quella, Fiordiligi! La Penelope,
L'Artemisia del secolo! Briccona,
Assassina, furfante, ladra, cagna!

113

DON ALFONSO
(*happily, aside*)

We'll let him blow off steam.	Lasciamolo sfogar.

FERRANDO
(*entering*)

Well, well!	Ebben!

GUGLIELMO

Well, what?	Dov'è?

FERRANDO

Well, your dear Fiordiligi?	Chi? la tua Fiordiligi?

GUGLIELMO

Oh, that one! Flower of the lily! The devil devour her,	La mia Fior . . . fior di diavolo, che strozzi
And me as well.	Lei prima a dopo me!

FERRANDO
(*ironically*)

We're in the same boat.	Tu vedi bene:
'Differences may perhaps have escaped you.	V'han delle differenze in ogni cosa.
I blame it all on Nature.'	Un poco più di merto . . .

GUGLIELMO

Oh, stop it! Let's put	Ah, cessa, cessa
Our heads together, admit we're both defeated,	Di tormentarmi; ed una via piuttosto
And think up some good way of	Studiam di castigarle
Retaliation.	Sonoramente.

DON ALFONSO

I tell you what: now marry them.	Io so qual è: sposarle.

GUGLIELMO

I would far sooner marry	Vorrei sposar piuttosto
The mother of the Gorgon.	La barca di Caronte.

FERRANDO

Or sleep in Vulcan's smithy.	La grotta di Vulcano.

GUGLIELMO

Surrounded by the Furies.	La porta dell'inferno.

DON ALFONSO

Would you remain a bachelor for ever?	Dunque, restate celibi in eterno.

FERRANDO

If I never discover	Mancheran forse donne
A woman who is worthy!	Ad uomin come noi?

DON ALFONSO

The girls have failed I grant you,	Non c'è abbondanza d'altro.
But how would others fare if those were wanting?	Ma l'altre che faran, se ciò fer queste?
Deep down, you do still love them,	In fondo, voi le amate
Although you have contrived to pluck their feathers.	Queste vostre cornacchie spennacchiate.

GUGLIELMO

I'm afraid so!	Ah, purtroppo!

FERRANDO

Afraid so!	Purtroppo!

114

DON ALFONSO

You must accept them	Ebben, pigliatele
As they really are. You boasted you had found	Com'elle son. Natura non potea
Paragons of Nature, but how should Nature	Fare l'eccezione, il privilegio
Have created for you two perfect beings	Di creare due donne d'altra pasta
In a generous moment? You were in error.	Per i vostri bei musi; in ogni cosa
Adopt a stoic posture, for we must figure	Ci vuol filosofia. Venite meco:
How this pretty masquerade	Di combinar le cose
Can be brought to completion.	Studierem la maniera.
I suggest that this evening	Vo' che ancor questa sera
We arrange a double wedding. But first though,	Doppie nozze si facciano. Frattanto,
I'll recite you an octave,	Un'ottava ascoltate:
And I trust it will temper your invective.	Felicissimi voi, se la imparate.

No. 30 Aria

DON ALFONSO

Men of course blame the ladies, but I excuse them	Tutto accusan le donne, ed io le scuso
And my indulgence never will refuse them.	Se mille volte al di cangiano amore;
Man's love is a passion, a life's anxiety,	Altri un vizio lo chiama ed altri un uso;
To her the charm is love's variety.	Ed a me par necessità del core.
The lover who, when he finds that he's deluded,	L'amante che si trova alfin deluso
Cannot blame her for that, the fault is Nature's;	Non condanni l'altrui, ma il proprio errore;
Be she youthful, aged, a scarecrow, a beauty!	Giacchè, giovani, vecchie, e belle e brutte,
Say the words after me: *Così fan tutte!*	Ripetete con me: *Così fan tutte!*

FERRANDO, GUGLIELMO AND DON ALFONSO

Così fan tutte!	*Così fan tutte!*

Scene Fourteen.* *Ferrando, Guglielmo, Don Alfonso and Despina. / Secco Recitative*

DESPINA
(entering)

Well, gentlemen, you've won them.	Vittoria, padroncini!
And my two pretty ladies	A sposarvi disposte
Are agreeable to marry you, and so I ventured	Son le care madame; a nome vostro
To promise them on your part you would be quite ready	Loro io promisi che in tre giorni circa
To start the honeymoon this evening. I must be off now	Partiranno con voi; l'ordin mi diero
In search of a notary	Di trovar un notaio
To draw up the marriage contract; meantime the ladies	Che stipuli il contratto; alla lor camera
Will be pleased to receive you.	Attendendo vi stanno.
Now, are you quite contented?	Siete così contenti?

FERRANDO, GUGLIELMO AND DON ALFONSO

Oh, abundantly!	Contentissimi.

DESPINA

Who Despina engages,	Non è mai senza effetto,
Will find she never fails to earn her wages!	Quand'entra la Despina in un progetto.

(They leave.)

---

* Often cut in performance.

Scene Fifteen. *A very luxurious and illuminated saloon with musicians at the back. A table laid for four persons, with silver cutlery etc.. Despina, servants, musicians and later Don Alfonso. / No. 31 Finale*

DESPINA
(to the servants)

Come, my friends, no more delaying. [17]
Hurry with your preparations,
Bring the table decorations,
Set it all in rich array.

Let us do our best to honour
An exceptional occasion.

(to the musicians)

For be sure a double wedding
Does not happen every day.

Fate presto, o cari amici,
Alle faci il fuoco date
E la mensa preparate
Con richezza e nobiltà.

Delle nostre padroncine
Gl'imenei son già disposti.

E voi gite ai vostri posti,
Finchè i sposi vengon qua.

CHORUS
(servants)

Let us help her, as she asks us,
With the special preparations,
And the table decorations
We will set in rich array.

Facciam presto, o cari amici,
Alle faci il fuoco diamo
E la mensa prepariamo
Con richezza e nobiltà.

DON ALFONSO
(entering)

Bravo, bravo! That's really splendid!
Nothing's wanting, it's enchanting!
A reward of fine proportions
Both the parties can afford.

Bravi, bravi! Ottimamente!
Che abbondanza! che eleganza!
Una mancia conveniente
L'un e l'altro a voi darà.

(While Don Alfonso sings, the musicians are tuning up.)

Very soon they will be entering,
Please applaud them on arrival.
Sing a festive song to greet them.
Fill the air with joyful sound.

Le due coppie omai si avanzano.
Fate plauso al loro arrivo:
Lieto canto e suon giulivo
Empia il ciel d'ilarità.

DESPINA AND DON ALFONSO
(sottovoce, leaving by separate doors)

It's a merry jest we've plotted
And absurd as any play!

La più bella commediola
Non s'è vista o si vedrà!

Scene Sixteen. *Fiordiligi, Dorabella, Ferrando, Guglielmo, servants and musicians. As the couples move forward, the chorus sings and the orchestra starts up a march.*

CHORUS

Now may love, that has united them, [18]
Bring delight beyond expressing!
May good fortune be benevolent,
And with every other blessing
Many offspring come to favour them,
Soon to equal them in joy!

Benedetti i doppi coniugi
E le amabili sposine!
Splenda lor il ciel benefico,
Ed a guisa di galline
Sien di figli ognor prolofiche,
Che le agguaglino in beltà.

FIORDILIGI, DORABELLA, FERRANDO AND GUGLIELMO

Feast and song are here combining,
Our unspoken wish divining!

Come par che qui prometta
Tutto gioia e tutto amore!

All, we know, is your designing:
Grateful thanks we owe to you!

Della cara Despinetta
Certo il merito sarà.

Raise again the welcome chorus,
Song and wine to joy restore us,
And the festive board before us
Shall resound with mirth and glee.

Raddoppiate il lieto suono,
Replicate il dolce canto,
E noi qui seggiamo intanto
In maggior giovialità.

CHORUS

May the love that has united them
With delight beyond expressing,

Benedetti i doppi coniugi
E le amabili sposine!

116

May good fortune be benevolent,	Splenda loro il ciel benefico,
And with every other blessing	Ed a guisa di galline
Many offspring come to favour them,	Sien di figli ognor prolifiche,
Soon to equal them in joy.	Che le agguaglino in beltà.

(The chorus leaves: four servants remain to serve the bridal couples, who seat themselves at the table.)

FERRANDO AND GUGLIELMO

On your charms, my new found treasure,	Tutto, tutto, o vita mia,
I shall never tire of gazing!	Al mio fuoco or ben risponde.

FIORDILIGI AND DORABELLA

In my veins I feel such pleasure,	Pel mio sangue l'allegria
With its power my sense amazing.	Cresce, cresce e si diffonde.

FERRANDO AND GUGLIELMO

You're enchanting.   Sei pur bella!

FIORDILIGI AND DORABELLA

You're delightful!   Sei pur vago!

FERRANDO AND GUGLIELMO

Eyes bewitching –   Che bei rai!

FIORDILIGI AND DORABELLA

– And lips inviting –   Che bella bocca!

FERRANDO, GUGLIELMO, FIORDILIGI AND DORABELLA
(touching the glasses with their lips)

Touching, sipping! Sipping, touching!   Tocca e bevi! Bevi e tocca!

FIORDILIGI, DORABELLA AND FERRANDO

In our eyes and our embraces,	E nel tuo, nel mio bicchiero
Let us banish all sorrow's traces.	Si sommerga ogni pensiero.

(The ladies drink.)

Tears of sorrow are no longer now remaining,	E non resti più memoria
Of the past the image fades.	Del passato, ai nostri cor.

GUGLIELMO
(aside)

Ah! I wish their drink were poisonous,	Ah, bevessero del tossico,
I wish that it would choke them!	Queste volpi senza onor!

Scene Seventeen. *Fiordiligi, Dorabella, Ferrando, Guglielmo and Don Alfonso; later Despina disguised as a notary.*

DON ALFONSO
(entering)

Happy lovers! Fate conniving	Miei signori, tutto è fatto:
Lends her aid to our contriving!	Col contratto nuziale
Soon the Notary arriving	Il notaio è sulle scale,
Ipso facto you shall see.	E, *ipso facto*, qui verrà.

FIORDILIGI, DORABELLA, FERRANDO AND GUGLIELMO

Bravo! bravo! Let him enter.   Bravo, bravo! Passi subito!

DON ALFONSO

I will call him. This is he.   Vo a chiamarlo. Eccolo qua.

DESPINA
(entering, and in a nasal voice)

Heaven pour its blessings o'er you!	Augurandovi ogni bene.
Ladies, here you see before you	Il notaio Beccavivi
Me, the lawyer, Baccalaureo,	Coll'usata a voi sen viene
Bearing the important deed;	Notarile dignità.

Which, with all its regulations,	E il contratto stipulato
Covenants and stipulations,	Colle regole ordinarie
By your kind permission sitting,	Nelle forme giudiziarie,
Slightly coughing, nought omitting,	Pria tossendo, poi sedendo,
I will now commence to read.	*Clara voce* leggerà.

FIORDILIGI, DORABELLA, FERRANDO, GUGLIELMO AND DON ALFONSO

Bravo, bravo, yes indeed!	Bravo, bravo, in verità!

DESPINA

By this contract here indited	Per contratto da me fatto,
Now in wedlock are united	Si congiunge in matrimonio
Fiordiligi to Leander,	Fiordiligi con Sempronio
Dorabella to Philander;	E con Tizio Dorabella,
Noble sisters of Ferrara,	Sua legittima sorella:
Gentlemen of South Albania,	Quelle, dame ferraresi;
Of their own free wills contracted;	Questi, nobili albanesi.
And for dowry 'tis enacted . . .	E, per dote e controdote . . .

FIORDILIGI, DORABELLA, FERRANDO AND GUGLIELMO

None is wanted, that's for granted.	Cose note, cose note!
As you make it we will take it,	Vi crediamo, ci fidiamo,
We will sign, no more delay!	Soscriviam: date pur qua.

(*Only the two ladies sign.*)

DESPINA AND DON ALFONSO

Bravo, bravo, that's the way.	Bravi, bravi, in verità!

(*The document is still in Don Alfonso's hand, when the loud sound of drums and singing is heard in the distance.*) [4]

CHORUS
(*off-stage*)

Oh, the soldier's life for me,	Bella vita militar!
Ever o'er new countries ranging,	Ogni dì si cangia loco,
Daily scene and fortune changing,	Oggi molto e doman poco,
Now on land and now on sea.	Ora in terra ed or sul mar.

FIORDILIGI, DORABELLA, DESPINA, FERRANDO AND GUGLIELMO

What's that noise? What are they singing?	Che rumor, che canto è questo?

DON ALFONSO

Wait awhile; I go and see.	State cheti; io vo a guardar.

(*He goes to the window.*)

Misericordia!	Misericordia!
Terror enthrals me!	Numi del cielo!
Day most unfortunate!	Che caso orribile!
Your danger appals me.	Io tremo! io gelo!
Here come your lovers.	Gli sposi vostri . . .

FIORDILIGI AND DORABELLA

Here come our lovers?	Lo sposo mio . . .

DON ALFONSO

Who left you sighing,	In questo istante
With joyful faces	Tornaro, oddio;
Again returning,	Ed all riva
Coming ashore.	Sbarcano già!

FIORDILIGI, DORABELLA, FERRANDO AND GUGLIELMO

How unpropitious!	Cosa mai sento!
Barbarous fortune,	Barbare stelle!
Why so malicious?	In tal momento
What can we do?	Che si farà?

(*The servants remove the table and the musicians leave hurriedly.*)

FIORDILIGI AND DORABELLA
(to their lovers)

You cannot stay here.	Presto, partite!

FERRANDO, GUGLIELMO, DESPINA AND DON ALFONSO

If they suspect us here?	Ma se $\begin{cases} \text{ci} \\ \text{li} \end{cases}$ veggono?

FIORDILIGI AND DORABELLA

Do not delay here!	Presto, fuggite!

FERRANDO, GUGLIELMO, DESPINA AND DON ALFONSO

If they detect us here.	Ma se $\begin{cases} \text{ci} \\ \text{li} \end{cases}$ incontrano?

(Don Alfonso leads Despina to another room.)

FIORDILIGI AND DORABELLA

Go and conceal yourselves,	Là, là; celatevi,
For goodness' sake.	Per carità.

(They lead their lovers to another room. They re-emerge, unseen, and leave.)

Now Heaven defend us!	Numi, soccorso!

DON ALFONSO

Do not alarm yourselves!	Rasserenatevi . . .

FIORDILIGI AND DORABELLA

Good fortune send us!	Numi, consiglio!

DON ALFONSO

But only calm yourselves . . .	Ritranquillatevi . . .

FIORDILIGI AND DORABELLA
(almost frantically)

Or what the end will be,	Chi dal periglio
Oh who can tell?	Ci salverà?

DON ALFONSO

I'll dare to promise you,	In me fidatevi:
All will go well.	Ben tutto andrà.

FIORDILIGI AND DORABELLA

O'er my heart what terrors hover!	Mille barbari pensieri
If the truth he now discover,	Tormentando il cor mi vanno:
Then his love for me is over,	Se discoprono l'inganno,
Ah, whatever would he do?	Ah, di noi che mai sarà!

Scene Eighteen. *Fiordiligi and Dorabella; Ferrando and Guglielmo with military cloaks and hats; Despina still in the adjacent room; Don Alfonso.*

FERRANDO AND GUGLIELMO

Joy once more now our sorrow replaces,	Sani e salvi, agli amplessi amorosi
As again we behold the dear faces,	Delle nostre fidissime amanti
And we offer our tender embraces,	Ritorniamo, di gioia esultanti,
Thus fidelity reaps its reward.	Per dar premio alla lor fedeltà.

DON ALFONSO

Powers above us! Guglielmo! Ferrando!	Giusti Numi! Guglielmo, Ferrando!
Oh what pleasure! Here? How so? And wherefore?	Oh, che giubilo! Qui? Come, e quando?

FERRANDO AND GUGLIELMO

Sudden orders decreed our returning,	Richiamati da regio contrordine,
And the joyful intelligence learning,	Pieno il cor di contento e di gaudio,

Back we hastened with eagerness burning,	Ritorniamo alle spose adorabili,
By our presence to end their alarms!	Ritorniamo alla vostra amistà.

GUGLIELMO
(to Fiordiligi)

Your complexion is pale, you are silent.	Ma cos'è quel pallor, quel silenzio?

FERRANDO
(to Dorabella)

And your eye is bedewed with a tear!	L'idol mio perchè mesto si sta?

DON ALFONSO

Now concealment is surely impossible.	Dal diletto confuse ed attonite,
They are sad though their lovers are here!	Mute mute si restano là.

FIORDILIGI AND DORABELLA
(aside)

Speak I dare not! My voice has deserted me.	Ah, che al labbro le voci mi mancano:
How I tremble with shame and with fear!	Se non moro, un prodigio sarà.

(The servants bring in a trunk.)

GUGLIELMO

This, my sword, pray let me leave it	Permettete che sia posto
In your dressing room as usual.	Quel baul in quella stanza . . .

(He goes out of the door through which Despina went and returns immediately.)

What the devil! A man in hiding.	Dei che veggio! Un uom nascosto?
It's a lawyer. How bizarre!	Un notaio! Qui che fa?

DESPINA
(entering hatless)

It's no lawyer here in hiding,	Nossignor, non è un notaio:
See the mystery revealing.	È Despina mascherata
From a masquerade returning	Che dal ballo or è tornata,
It's Despina you see here!	E a spogliarsi venne qua.

(aside)

Yes, it's me and where my equal	Una furba che m'agguagli
For contrivance will you see?	Dove mai si troverà?

FERRANDO AND GUGLIELMO
(aside)

It's Despina, now the sequel	Una furba uguale a questa
Very quickly we shall see!	Dove mai si troverà?

(Don Alfonso cunningly lets fall the contract.)

FIORDILIGI AND DORABELLA

It's Despina but the sequel	La Despina! La Despina!
Is a mystery to me!	Non capisco come va.

DON ALFONSO
(sottovoce to the men)

There's the contract if you need it.	Già cader lasciai le carte:
Why not pick it up and read it?	Raccoglietele con arte.

FERRANDO
(recovering the contract)

What's this document I see here?	Ma che carte sono queste?

GUGLIELMO

It's a double marriage contract!	Un contratto nuziale?

FERRANDO AND GUGLIELMO
(to the ladies)

O ye gods, vain is denial,	Giusto ciel! Voi qui scriveste:
For the signatures condemn you.	Contraddirci omai non vale!

Oh disgrace beyond conception!	Tradimento, tradimento!
Wicked treason and deception!	Ah, si faccia il scoprimento,
Let us find the hateful rivals!	E a torrenti, a fiumi, a mari
Let our vengeance on them fall!	Indi il sangue scorrerà!

(They move to go into the other room but the ladies stop them.)

FIORDILIGI AND DORABELLA

Ah! My love, now let me perish,	Ah, signor, son rea di morte,
Hope of life no more I cherish.	E la morte io sol vi chiedo.
Shame, remorse and terrors fill me.	Il mio fallo tardi vedo:
With your sabre, unflinching, kill me!	Con quel ferro un sen ferite
Spare me not, I own it all!	Che non merita pietà.

FERRANDO AND GUGLIELMO

What is this?   Cosa fu?

FIORDILIGI AND DESPINA
(pointing at Don Alfonso and Despina)

| Ah! They can tell you! | Per noi favelli |
| 'Twas through them this woe befell us! | Il crudel, la seduttrice . . . |

DON ALFONSO

| It is useless to dissemble, | Troppo vero è quel che dice, |
| All the proof you need is there! | E la prova è chiusa lì. |

(He indicates the room which the suitors had previously entered, and Ferrando and Guglielmo go in.)

FIORDILIGI AND DORABELLA
(aside)

| Oh, with fear I faint and trepidate. | Dal timor io gelo, io palpito: |
| Why did he his friends betray? | Perchè mai li discopri! |

(Ferrando and Guglielmo come out of the room without hats, cloaks and moustaches, but in Albanian costume; they tease their lovers and Despina in a ridiculous way.)

FERRANDO
(paying exaggerated compliments to Fiordiligi)

Maiden so charming,	A voi s'inchina,
Quickly disarming	Bella damina,
A cavalier from	Il cavaliere
The wilds of Albania!	Dell' Albania!

GUGLIELMO
(to Dorabella, returning the miniature)

See here a treasure,	Il ritrattino
Guarded with pleasure,	Per coricino,
Yours in return, love,	Ecco, io le rendo,
Render to me.	Signora mia.

In its simplicity	Ed al magnetico
This great invention,	Signor dottore
This mighty mystery,	Rendo l'onore
Was all our own.	Che meritò.

FIORDILIGI, DORABELLA AND DESPINA

Wonder on wonder!   Stelle! Che veggo!

FERRANDO, GUGLIELMO AND DON ALFONSO

They are astounded!   Son stupefatte!

FIORDILIGI, DORABELLA AND DESPINA

Blunder on blunder!   Al duol non reggo!

FERRANDO, GUGLIELMO AND DON ALFONSO

They are confounded!   Son mezze matte!

FIORDILIGI AND DORABELLA
(indicating Don Alfonso)

Yet all our woes are due	Ecco là il barbaro
To him alone.	Che c'ingannò!

DON ALFONSO

True the plot was my invention	V'ingannai, ma fu l'inganno
And effected my intention:	Disinganno ai vostri amanti,
I desired but to persuade them	Che più saggi omai saranno,
Nothing's perfect here below!	Che faran quel ch'io vorrò.

(He makes them unite and embrace.)

So forgiving, be united,	Qua le destre: siete sposi.
And above all else don't discuss it.	Abbracciatevi e tacete.
Now you all must laugh it off,	Tutti quattro ora ridete,
For there is nothing else to do.	Ch'io già risi e riderò.

FIORDILIGI AND DORABELLA

Ah, my love, if you'll accept it	Idol mio, se questo è vero,
Far more faithful than vows I've broken	Colla fede e coll'amore
Is my penitence, believe me,	Compensar saprò il tuo core,
As my future life will show!	Adorarti ognor saprò.

FERRANDO AND GUGLIELMO

I'll believe the word you've spoken,	Te lo credo, gioia bella,
To the proof no more I'll go.	Ma la prova io far non vo'.

DESPINA

The effect of my deception	Io non so se questo è sogno:
Is beyond all comprehension	Mi confondo, mi vergogno.
And indeed I've learned a lesson	Manco mal, se a me l'han fatta,
With a moral that is true.	Che a molt'altri anch'io la fo.
Take good care if fooling others	Manco mal, se a me l'han fatta,
Someone else may well fool you.	Che a molt'altri anch'io la fo.

FIORDILIGI, DORABELLA, DESPINA, FERRANDO, GUGLIELMO AND DON ALFONSO

Happy is the man who calmly	Fortunato l'uom che prende
Takes life strictly as he finds it.	Ogni cosa pel buon verso,
And with humour and patience only	E tra i casi e le vicende
Lets sweet reason be his guide.	Da ragion guidar si fa.
Fortune's frown can ne'er confound him;	Quel che suole altrui far piangere
He will smile at all around him	Fia per lui cagion di riso;
And despite each new calamity	E del mondo in mezzo ai turbini
He'll preserve a tranquil mind.	Bella calma troverà.

Curtain.

Graziella Sciutti as Despina and Geraint Evans as Don Alfonso at Covent Garden in 1972 (photo: Donald Southern)

Covent Garden 1968: left to right, Luigi Alva (Ferrando), Pilar Lorengar (Fiordiligi), Lucia Popp (Despina in disguise), Josephine Veasey (Dorabella) and Wladimiro Ganzarolli (Guglielmo) (photo: Houston Rogers)

Note on 'Rivolgete a lui'

John Stone

Guglielmo's present first act aria *'Non siate ritrosi'* (No. 15) is a replacement for a more ambitious number 'Rivolgete a lui', the text of which is printed below. Analysis of the score in relation to evidence from Mozart's autograph provided by Alan Tyson suggests an interesting reason for the substitution. Mozart was apparently looking for an even distribution of keys in the act — two numbers to each key utilised — and the key of D major had been allotted to Guglielmo's aria and to the finale. However he discovered subsequently that he would be allowed a chorus and therefore wrote *'Bella vita militar'* (No. 8) — also in D — with a new ending for *'Di scrivermi'* (No. 9) to link up with its *da capo*/ repetition. In order to maintain the balance he scrapped *'Rivolgete a lui'* and wrote *'Non siate ritrosi'* which being in G forms a single number with the trio *'E voi ridete'* (No. 16) that follows it.

No. 15 Aria

GUGLIELMO
(*to Fiordiligi*)

Fairest, see who stands before you	Rivolgete a lui lo sguardo
And to him your heart incline;	E vedrete come sta;
He is thinking: 'I love you, adore you,	Tutto dice: 'Io gelo . . . io ardo . . .
Goddess fair be mine, be mine.'	Idol mio, pietà, pietà!'

(*to Dorabella*)

You my dearest, be not angry,	E voi, cara, un sol momento
Turn your gaze for just a moment,	Il bel ciglio a me volgete,
In my eyes observe the torment	E nel mio ritroverete
That my lips dare not define.	Quel che il labbro dir non sa.
All the passion of Orlando	Un Orlando innamorato
Could not be more Furioso,	Non è niente, in mio confronto;
All the wounds of sad Medoro	D'un Medoro il sen piagato
Count for nought, as mind bleed more so:	Verso lui per nulla io conto:
Fanned by sighs my fires are burning,	Son di fuoco i miei sospiri,
Hard as bronze his love is turning.	Son di bronzo i suoi desiri.
Should you wish to speak of talent,	Se si parla poi di merto,
There is none in men so gallant	Certo io sono, ed egli è certo,
To be found in such a quantity	Che gli uguali non si trovano
From Vienna to Cathay:	Da Vienna al Canadà:
We are both as rich as Croesus,	Siam due cresi per ricchezza,
Beautiful as fair Narcissus.	Due narcisi per bellezza;
Lovers we, as good as any,	In amor i Marcantoni
Far outclassing Don Giovanni;	Verso noi sarian buffoni.
We are stronger than the Cyclops	Siam più forti d'un Ciclopo,
And tell taller tales than Aesop's,	Letterati al par di Esopo;
At a ball we know no equal,	Se balliamo, un Pich* ne cede,
Feather-light at every footfall.	Si gentil e snello è il piede;

* 'Pick is the famous dancer, Le Pick, who took part in a ballet-intermezzo by the young Mozart *Le gelosie del serraglio* in Milan, in the summer of 1771.

When we sing the notes come streaming,	Se cantiam, col trillo solo
Set the nightingales a'dreaming.	Facciam torto al lusignuolo;
Other matters I could mention,	E qualch'altro capitale
Maybe on another day.	Abbiam, poi, che alcun. non sa.

(*The ladies leave in a fury.*)

Paragons of stern resistance,	Bella, bella! Tengon sodo;
They retreat but we are vanquished;	Se ne vanno, ed io ne godo!
Heroines of resolution,	Eroine di costanza,
Mirrors of fidelity.	Specci son di fedeltà.

(*Ferrando and Guglielmo begin to laugh uproariously.*)

Thomas Allen as Guglielmo at Covent Garden in 1981 (photo: Clive Barda)

Discography by *Martin Hoyle.* For detailed analysis the enthusiast is referred to *Opera on Record*, ed. Alan Blyth, Hutchinson 1979.

Conductor Orchestra/Opera House	*Boehm* Philharmonia	*Solti* LPO	*Davis* Royal Opera	*Boehm* VPO
Fiordiligi	Schwarzkopf	Lorengar	Caballé	Janowitz
Dorabella	Ludwig	Berganza	Baker	Fassbaender
Despina	Steffek	Berbié	Cotrubas	Grist
Ferrando	Kraus	Davies	Gedda	Schreier
Guglielmo	Taddei	Krause	Ganzarolli	Prey
Don Alfonso	Berry	Bacquier	Van Allan	Panerai
Disc UK	SLS 5028	D56D4	6707 025	2709 059
Tape UK	TC-SLS 5028	–	7699 055	3371 019
Excerpts UK (disc)	SXLP 30457	–	6570 099	2537 037
Excerpts UK (tape)	TC-SXLP 30457	–	7310 099	–
Disc US	Angel S 3631	Lon 1442	6707 025	2709 059
Tape US	–	–	7699 134	3371 019
Excerpts US (disc)	Angel S 36167	–	–	2537 037
Excerpts US (tape)	–	–	–	3306 037

Conductor	Lombard	Suitner	Busch	Stiedry
Orchestra/Opera House	Strasbourg PO	Berlin State Opera	Glyndebourne	NY Metropolitan
Fiordiligi	Te Kanawa	Casapietra	Souez	Steber
Dorabella	von Stade	Burmeister	Helletsgruber	Thebom
Despina	Stratas	Geszty	Eisinger	Peters
Ferrando	Rendall	Schreier	Nash	Tucker
Guglielmo	Huttenlocher	Leib	Domgraf-Fassbaender	Guarrera
Don Alfonso	Bastin	Adam	Brownlee	Alvary
Disc UK	STU 71110	80408 XGR	–	–
Tape UK	–	500 213	–	–
Disc US	–	80408	SERA 6127; THS-65126	Y-3-32670
Tape US	–	–	SERA 6127	–

Excerpts: Jurinac, Thebom, Lewis, Kunz, Boriello; Glyndebourne/Busch   SH 397 (disc UK)

Bibliography

Alfred Einstein's *Mozart, his Character, his Work* (London, 1969), which covers Mozart's life and other compositions besides his operas, is a compact, readable and immensely perceptive general study. The controversial biography by Wolfgang Hildesheimer (trans. M. Faber, London, 1983) is also highly recommended for a survey of all the operas which contains many insights into *Così* in particular. There are individual longer chapters in the classic by E.J. Dent, *Mozart's Operas: A Critical Study* (London 1913, 1947) and *The Operas of Mozart* by William Mann (London 1977). Charles Rosen discusses the opera in a brief but illuminating passage in *The Classical Style* (1971, Faber Paperback 1980).

Emily Anderson's translation of *The Letters of Mozart and his Family* (3 vols, London, 1938) contains the desperate begging letters written around the time of the composition of *Così*. Arthur Hutchins's beautifully illustrated *Mozart* (London, 1976) provides charming visual background material of the period.

The only English biography of da Ponte is by April FitzLyon *Lorenzo da Ponte* (London, 1982). His *Memorie*, translated by Elisabeth Abbott (Philadelphia, 1929), make fascinating reading. The chapter in Patrick J. Smith's *The Tenth Muse: A Historical Study of the Opera Libretto* (London, 1971) is the best survey of contemporary librettos.

Ariosto's *Orlando Furioso* (trans. Guido Waldman) is published in *The World's Classics* series of Oxford Paperbacks (1983). Ovid's *Metamorphoses* (trans. Mary Innes, 1955) is available in Penguin Classics.

Contributors

Brian Trowell is King Edward Professor of Music at King's College London.

H.C. Robbins Landon is John Bird Visiting Professor of Music at University College, Cardiff, and the author of a 5-volume *Life of Haydn*.

John Stone is currently working on a study of Mozart and his cultural background.

John Cox is Artistic Director of Scottish Opera.